THE BATTLE OF
CLONMULT

THE BATTLE OF CLONMULT

THE IRA'S WORST DEFEAT

REVISED EDITION

TOM O'NEILL M.A.

The History Press

This book is dedicated to my wife, Ann, and our sons, Finbarr and Philip.
Thanks for the support and patience.

First Published 2006 by Nonsuch Publishing Ltd
This paperback revised edition first published 2019

The History Press
97 St George's Place, Cheltenham,
Gloucestershire, GL50 3QB
www.thehistorypress.co.uk

British Library Cataloguing in Publication Data.
A catalogue record for this book is available from the British Library.

ISBN 978 0 7509 9221 3

Typesetting and origination by Geethik Technologies and The History Press
Printed and bound by TJ International Ltd.

CONTENTS

ACKNOWLEDGEMENTS

The research and completion of this, the second edition of *The Battle of Clonmult*, would not have been possible without the co-operation, assistance and support of a number of individuals. Mr Gabriel Doherty was my supervisor in University College Cork for my MA thesis in Local History, for which 'The Battle of Clonmult', was my chosen subject. I want to thank him for his guidance, advice and encouragement. To Mai Kerins must go a very special thanks for her invaluable work in proofreading the text of both editions of this book.

I wish to thank the Officer Commanding, Irish Military Archives, Cathal Brugha Barracks, Dublin and his staff, for their efficiency in producing copies of the Bureau of Military History, Witness Statements. I wish to thank the staff of the reference department of the National Library of Ireland, Dublin, and in particular Mr Tom Desmond. Thanks also to the staff of the Cork Archive Institute, and the Special Collections Dept., (Q–1), U.C.C. To Mr Dan Breen, acting curator of the Cork City Public Museum, Fitzgerald Park, for locating some of the original Clonmult photographs and to Mr Brian McGee, chief archivist, and the staff of the Cork City and County Archives for their assistance.

In East Cork I am grateful to the following for supplying information: the late Miss Mary Murnane, daughter of Volunteer Mick Murnane, the late Miss Eimer Burke, daughter of Capt Michael Burke and niece of Capt James Ahern, killed in action at Clonmult. Thanks to Miss Ursula O'Mahony of Ballinacurra and the Cloyne Historical Society. My thanks to Ms Anne McAuliffe, widow of the late Mr John McAuliffe, for allowing me to use original photographs from her late husband's collection. I am also indebted to Mr John Mulcahy of Whitechurch, County Cork, for locating the British Army reports of the battle – these had been misfiled at the United Kingdom National Archives (UKNA), London – and to Mr John Arnold.

It was a privilege to interview the late Mr Jim Hegarty, a native of Clonmult and a witness to the battle. Many thanks also to Miss Pauline Cotter for arranging the interviews with her late mother, Mrs Theresa Cotter. Thanks to the late Mr Tomás O Riordán for providing some valuable information. To my brother, Vincent, for his involvement in the Battle of Clonmult lectures.

In addition to those already mentioned I wish to add the following for their assistance, advice and support: Mr Eugene Power, Mr Donal Vaughan, and Mr Gerry White for directing me to the Clonmult Military Court case file. A special thanks to Dr Andrew Bielenberg, Senior Lecturer, UCC History Department for sending me the details of the Military Court of Inquiry in lieu of an inquest, the Patrick Higgins lecture and the Clonmult details in the Mulcahy Papers. To Dr Gillian O'Brien, Reader in Modern Irish History, Liverpool John Moores University, and Dr Daithi O Corrain, Lecturer in History, School of History and Geography, DCU. To Lt Col Colin Bulleid, secretary of the The Royal Hampshire Regiment Trust, Winchester, UK, for providing some information from the British military side and for the photographs of some of the members of the Hampshire Regiment involved in the battle.

Many thanks to my fellow members of the Clonmult Ambush Commemoration Committee: chairman Christy O'Sullivan, secretary Tim O'Sullivan, treasurer Sean Hennessy, assistant treasurer Jim O'Callaghan, assistant secretary John Walsh, also Mary Barron, Cllr Michael Hegarty, Michael Hegarty, Clonmult, Cllr Michael Ahern and Jim Ronayne.

To my son, Finbarr O'Neill, for providing the support for the digitalisation of images and maps.

All of these individuals have helped me in the course of my research into this work. Any errors or omissions are entirely mine.

Very special thanks to Christy O'Sullivan and his wife, Geraldine, the owners and guardians of the site of the Battle of Clonmult. Their enthusiasm and hospitality towards all callers is fantastic.

Finally, I hope that anyone whose copyright my book has unwittingly infringed will accept my sincere apology.

LIST OF ABBREVIATIONS

A.S.U.	Active Service Unit
C.B.	Companion of the Order of the Bath
C.C.	Catholic Curate
CO	Commanding Officer
Col	Colonel
Comdt	Commandant, Irish equivalent of a British Army major
C.I.	County Inspector (RIC)
CSM	Company Sergeant Major
D.I.	District Inspector (RIC)
Div	Division
D.S.O.	Distinguished Service Order
Gen	General
G.H.Q.	General Headquarters
I.G.	Inspector General (RIC)
I.O.	Intelligence Officer
IRA	Irish Republican Army
Lt	Lieutenant
Lt Col	Lieutenant-Colonel
M.B.E.	Member of the Order of the British Empire
M.C.	Military Cross (bravery medal)
M.M.	Military Medal (bravery medal)
OC	Officer Commanding
QM Officer	Quartermaster Officer
RIC	Royal Irish Constabulary
T.C.I.	Temporary County Inspector (RIC)
Vol	Volunteer

REVOLUTIONARY CORK

This chapter briefly covers in chronological sequence the political and military events, both national and local, from January 1913 to February 1921 that led to the Battle of Clonmult. It also introduces the individuals who were involved in the Flying Column of the 4th Battalion, First Cork Brigade IRA, the unit involved at Clonmult. It was the men of these flying columns, using the appropriate strategy, with a political mandate based on the results of the General Election of 1918 and on the material support of the people that made the War of Independence possible.

A public meeting to formally establish the Irish Volunteers was held in the Rotunda Rink in Dublin on the night of 25th November 1913, presided over by Eoin MacNeill.[1] The public meeting that inaugurated the Irish Volunteers in Cork City and county was held in the old Cork City Hall, at 8.30 pm, on the evening of Sunday, 14th December 1913.[2] The principal speakers were Eoin MacNeill and Sir Roger Casement, while also in attendance was Tomás MacCurtain, officer commanding the First Cork Brigade and the future Lord Mayor of Cork. During the first six months of 1914, a Volunteer Company was set up in Cobh that was one of the first in what became the 4th Battalion area.[3]

Following the outbreak of the First World War in August 1914, the leader of the Irish Parliamentary Party, John Redmond MP, in a speech in Woodenbridge County Wicklow on 20th September 1914, proposed that members of the Irish Volunteers should militarily support Britain in its hour of need and by doing so would help end the war and thus ensure that Home Rule would be obtained.

---

1   Gerry White & Brendan O'Shea, *Baptised in Blood*, Mercier Press, 2005, p. 13.
2   Florence O'Donoghue, *Tomás MacCurtain*, p. 14.
3   *Ibid*. p. 20.

This led to a split in the Irish Volunteers. The majority, approximately 170,000, followed John Redmond and this group became known as the National or Redmond's Volunteers and many enlisted in the British Forces. The remainder, approximately 12,000, retained the title and principles of the Irish Volunteers.[4]

Jack O'Connell, the acting column commander at Clonmult, was originally a member of the Irish Volunteers. After the split of September 1914, he joined Redmond's National Volunteers and in March 1915 he re-joined the Irish Volunteers.[5] Other men from Cobh who were active in the Volunteer movement from this period were Paddy Whelan, involved at Clonmult, Daithi O'Brien, (OC) officer commanding 'A' (Cobh) Company during the War of Independence, Michael Leahy who became (CO) commanding officer of the 4th Battalion and James Ahern, killed at Clonmult.[6]

During Easter week of 1916, the Volunteers were mobilised at Sheares Street in Cork City. Their mission was to act as security for the distribution of the arms and ammunition that they were expecting from the gun-running ship 'Aud'. However, as a result of the capture of the 'Aud' off the Kerry coast on Good Friday evening by a Royal Navy warship and later its scuttling outside the entrance to Cork Harbour early on Easter Saturday morning, all the awaited weapons and ammunition were lost, therefore the men returned to the city empty-handed. Also, because of conflicting orders from Dublin and a lack of direct communications with their superiors in the city, the Cork units did not play an active part in the Rising of Easter Week.

In the immediate post-1916 Rising period the British authorities made at least two major errors. Firstly, they executed the leaders and overnight turned these men into martyrs. Secondly, they interned 1,863 of the insurgents in a disused distillery and former prisoner of war camp in Frongoch, North Wales.[7] This internment camp has been aptly described as 'a university of revolution'.[8] This in my opinion was the greater error because it brought together many of the leading individuals of the War of Independence. Michael Brennan of Clare, Michael Collins, Tomás MacCurtain and Terence MacSwiney of Cork, Michael Leahy of Cobh,[9] Tom McEllistrim of Kerry, Dick McKee, Dick Mulcahy and Sean T. O'Kelly of Dublin, to name but a few.

---

4   Gerry White & Brendan O'Shea, *Irish Volunteer Soldier 1913–23*, pp. 5 and 9.
5   Lt Col Jack O'Connell, *Witness Statement (WS) No. 1367*, p. 1.
6   Michael Leahy, *WS No. 94*, p. 1.
7   Sean O'Mahony, *Frongoch: University of Revolution*.
8   *Ibid.*
9   *Ibid.* p. 172.

It was at Frongoch that the lessons of the Rising were debated, the mistakes identified and the strategies and tactics of the War of Independence decided. It was decided that never again would they take on the might of the Crown Forces using conventional warfare.[10] The next war would be one of guerrilla actions, no more taking over buildings and waiting to be attacked. It was at Frongoch that it was recognised that priority must be given to destroying the Royal Irish Constabulary, a force that was seen as the eyes and ears of Dublin Castle in every corner of Ireland and also the 'G' Division of the Dublin Metropolitan Police. The network of contacts that was essential for conducting a national resistance movement was forged during the long period of internment in North Wales. This camaraderie was the driving force that propelled the Irish Republican Army during the War of Independence, 1917–21, a period described by the volunteers as the four glorious years.[11]

An Irish Volunteer Company was formed in Midleton towards the end of 1916. Jack O'Shea, John Brady and Sean Buckley were the Company officers.[12] Towards the end of 1917, the 4th Battalion companies were redesignated and Cobh became 'A' Company and Midleton became 'B' Company.

Paddy Higgins, wounded at Clonmult, was the first Company captain of 'L' Company in Aghada and remained in that appointment until late 1918 when he was reapointed 4th Battalion (QM) quarter-master officer.[13] He joined the battalion flying column during December 1920. Joseph Ahern, later second-in-command of the flying column, was active in the Volunteers in Midleton from the earliest days.[14] Joseph Ahern was the commanding officer of the 4th Battalion at the Truce. The Midleton Company parade ground was a walled enclosure in an old ruined castle yard at Cahermone, a short distance on the east side of the town. Their rifles were 'stout branches broken off nearby trees'.[15] Diarmuid O'Hurley from Kilbrittan, west Cork and column commander at Clonmult, arrived in Midleton from Belfast in September 1918. Diarmuid O'Hurley worked as a foreman in T.S.R. Coppinger, grain merchants, on Main Street. It was here that he received the nickname 'The Gaffer'. He was soon after appointed OC of the Midleton Company.[16] Paddy Whelan, originally

10 Michael Hopkinson, *The War of Independence*, p. 13.
11 David Hogan, (pseudo. Frank Gallagher), *The Four Glorious Years*.
12 John Kelleher, *WS No. 1456*, p. 1.
13 Paddy Higgins, *WS No. 1467*, p. 2.
14 Joseph Ahern, *WS No. 1367*, p. 2.
15 *Ibid*.
16 Tomás O'Riordán, 'Diarmuid O'Hurley', in, *Imokilly People Newspaper*, 7th June 2001, p. 15.

from Wexford, moved to Cobh where his father was employed by Irish Lights and worked on the Daunt Rock lightship. Paddy began work as a boilermaker's apprentice in His Majesty's Dockyard, Haulbowline, in September 1914.[17] Paddy Whelan, Jeremiah Ahern and Jack O'Connell, worked in the Midleton Engineering Works, prior to joining the column. Joseph Morrissey, born in Carlow and later living in Roscommon and on the run from the Midlands, worked in Abernethy's Bakery in Castlemartyr.

Up to 5th January 1919, the area of operations of the First Cork Brigade covered all of County Cork.[18] On that date at a meeting held at Kilnadur, Dunmanway, and chaired by Michael Collins – who was representing G.H.Q. – the county was divided into three brigade areas as it was proving almost impossible to command and administer.[19] The First Cork Brigade's new and reduced area of operations covered the city, west to Ballingeary and east to Youghal with Tomás MacCurtain, later Lord Mayor of Cork City, as brigade commander. The 2nd Brigade covered north Cork with Liam Lynch in charge, and the 3rd (West Cork) Brigade under Tom Hales covered the western part of the county to the Kerry border.

There were ten battalions numbered 1 to 10 in the 1st Brigade. The activities covered in this book relate primarily to the Flying Column of the 4th Battalion, Cork 1st Brigade, Irish Republican Army. The territorial boundary of the 4th Battalion corresponded roughly with the old Parliamentary area of East Cork. The western boundary extended from Dunkettle Bridge adjacent to the northern entrance to the Jack Lynch Tunnel, north through Glanmire to Knockraha. The northern boundary was from Knockraha, east through Leamlara, Ballincurrig, Clonmult, Inch, Killeagh to Youghal. The southern boundary was the coastline from Youghal back to Dunkettle Bridge and including the Great Island.[20]

There were seventeen Companies in the 4th Battalion with a strength of more than 1,200 men.[21] The Companies of the 4th Battalion were designated by a capital letter and were as follows. 'A' Company Cobh, 'B' Company Midleton, 'C' Company Youghal, 'D' Company Carrigtwohill, 'E' Company Knockraha, 'F' Company Dungourney, Clonmult, Mogeely and Castlemartyr, 'G' Company Lisgoold, 'H' Company Leamlara, 'I' Company Ladysbridge, 'J'

17   Patrick Whelan, *WS No. 1449*, p. 1.
18   Florence O'Donoghue, Tomás MacCurtain, p. 151.
19   *Ibid.*
20   Joseph Ahern, *WS No. 1367*, p. 1.
21   Seamus Fitzgerald, 'East Cork Activities – 1920', in, *The Capuchin Annual 1970*, Dublin, p. 360.

Company Inch and Killeagh, 'K' Company Cloyne, 'L' Company Aghada, 'M' Company Shanagarry, 'N' Company Ballycotton, 'O' Company Ballymacoda, 'P' Company Glounthaune, 'R' Company Churchtown South.

In 1921, during the Truce, a number of the Companies were detached from the 4th Battalion and redesignated 10th Battalion. These became 'A' Company Aghada, 'B' Company Cloyne, 'C' Company Churchtown South, 'D' Company Shanagarry, 'E' Company Ballycotton, 'F' Company Ladysbridge, 'G' Company Ballymacoda, 'H' Company Killeagh, 'I' Company Inch, 'J' Company Gortroe and 'K' Company Youghal, 10th Battalion, First Cork Brigade.

One of the priorities of all active Companies throughout the War of Independence was that of acquiring arms and ammunition. The IRA obtained their weapons from a variety of sources. Initially, the Volunteers raided private houses and gun shops in their search for firearms, but this proved successful only to a point, as the types of weapons procured generally only amounted to shotguns and .22in rifles, which were quite useless against service .303in rifles.[22] Their main focus for weapons was on the Crown Forces because service rifles, revolvers and ammunition were their main requirement. A fruitful source of service rifles were the Irishmen who were home on leave from the British Army. If the individual was lucky, he was asked to sell the rifle but often there was no choice. The authorities soon cut off this source when armouries were made available in England to secure the rifles of soldiers travelling home on leave to Ireland.

The General Election of December 1918 was a political turning point for Sinn Féin and the Republican movement. For these Nationalists it was a battle between the old Parliamentary Party and Sinn Féin. Of the seventy-three Republican candidates, forty-seven were in jail. The Sinn Féin election slogan was, 'Vote them in to get them out'. The result of the election was a resounding victory for Sinn Féin. Of the 105 candidates returned for Ireland, seventy-three were Sinn Féin, twenty-six were Loyalist and just six for the Parliamentary Party.[23] The elected Republicans refused to take their seats at Westminster and instead formed the First Dáil, which met in the Mansion House in Dublin on 21st January 1919. The Dáil adopted three foundation deeds, of which the 'Declaration of Independence' was the one of greatest importance to the IRA.[24]

---

22   Kieran McCarthy and Maj-Britt Christensen, *Cobh's Contribution to the Fight for Irish Freedom 1913–1990*, pp. 28–34.

23   David Hogan, *The Four Glorious Years*, p. 55.

24   Charles Townshend, *The British Campaign in Ireland, 1919–1921, The Development of Political and Military Policies*, p. 15.

This declared 'that a state of war existed which could never end until Ireland is definitely evacuated by the armed forces of England'.[25]

The Deputies standing, affirmed, 'we adopt this Declaration of Independence, and we pledge ourselves to put it into effect by every means in our power'.[26]

The principal means in their power was the IRA, and this 'Declaration of Independence' was seen by the organisation as a mandate from the majority of the Irish people, through the Dáil, for its military campaign against the British Forces. This was the basis for their claim that they were the soldiers of the Irish Republic. In the eyes of those involved there was now an Irish political establishment with a military force ready for the impending war. The first fatal shots of that war were heard in Soloheadbeg, Co. Tipperary, the very same day as the First Dáil sat. Two RIC constables, James McDonnell from Mayo and Patrick O'Connell from Coachford, Co. Cork, were shot dead in an ambush at Soloheadbeg by the men of the Third Tipperary Brigade.[27]

The men most active in the movement between 1918 and mid-1920 were part-time. They worked at their civilian employment during the day, assembled for a raid or attack during the night or weekend and returned to their work the following morning. These early raids were quite successful as they generally had the element of surprise. The men involved at Clonmult were active in most of these operations.

Some of the early successes in East Cork included:

The capture and destruction of the Carrigtwohill RIC Barracks on 3rd January 1920, one of the first such successes in the country.

The capture of Castlemartyr RIC Barracks on 9th February 1920.

A British Army patrol disarmed near Cobh, one soldier killed.

The capture of Cloyne RIC Barracks on 8th May 1920.

The disarming of the joint British Army/RIC bicycle patrol at Mile Bush near Midleton on Saturday, 5th June 1920. Twelve rifles captured.

---

25   *Ibid.*
26   Dorothy Macardle, *The Irish Republic*, p. 274.
27   Dan Breen, *My Fight for Irish Freedom*, pp. 38–58, also, Richard Abbott, Police Casualties in Ireland 1919–1922, pp. 30–33.

A British Army guard disarmed near Cobh on 25th August 1920, one soldier killed.[28]

A British Army mobile patrol attacked at Whiterock, outside Midleton on 26th August 1920, one soldier killed.

However, the authorities were building up intelligence on the activists and quite a few were arrested. The remainder, knowing they had been identified and were wanted, went 'on the run'. Tadhg Manley and Diarmuid O'Hurley were lodging at Mrs Walsh's, 70 Chapel St., now St Mary's Rd., in Midleton. A party of Cameron Highlanders raided the house on Monday, 7th June 1920, two days after the Mile Bush ambush. Tadhg Manley was captured and O'Hurley only just managed to escape out through the back door.[29] Tadhg Manley spent the remainder of the war in jail.

The introduction of the Restoration of Order in Ireland Act on 9th August 1920 forced more men on the run. The authorities were finding it almost impossible to find jurors and this Act introduced internment without trial. It was a natural progression that those 'on the run' who were often living in the same safe houses would eventually band together and this was the birth of the concept of the flying columns.

About this time, Ernie O'Malley,[30] Divisional Commander of the Second Southern Division, stated that, 'at the time and for sometime later, the men on the run were a bloody nuisance, for they lounged around, slept late, ate people's food and did no work for the company or battalion in whom they happened to be'.[31] However, the formation of the flying columns, which involved training and discipline, established these men into an effective fighting force.

Towards the end of September 1920, the 4th Battalion Flying Column was formed at Knockraha, approximately six kilometres east of Cork City, under the command of Diarmuid O'Hurley. Joseph Ahern, Jack Ahern, brothers David and Michael Desmond, Michael Hallahan and Paddy Whelan were the first to report for duty.[32] Michael Hallahan resided in number 12 and the two Desmond brothers resided in number 17 Commissioners Buildings in Midleton. The terrace was later renamed Clonmult Terrace in memory of these three men killed

---

28 *Rebel Corks Fighting Story*, pp. 179–189.
29 Patrick Whelan, *WS No. 1449*, p. 29.
30 Padraig O'Farrell, *Who's Who in the Irish War of Independence*, p. 128.
31 U.C.D., A.D., *O'Malley Papers*, p. 17 b/114.
32 Paddy Whelan, *WS No. 1449*, pp. 35–36.

at Clonmult. These men were the full-time members of the column from its formation until Clonmult. For a list of the other men known to have served in the flying column, see Appendix 4, pp. 120–21.

The nature of the terrain around East Cork did not lend itself to the security of a large flying column. The terrain was too well served with roads and there were military garrisons at Cobh, Midleton, Youghal, Fermoy, Cork and Fort Carlisle near Whitegate. The average number serving on the column at any one time was generally kept to between sixteen and twenty. There were, however, many men who were available at short notice to reinforce the column.[33] The rugged terrain of West Cork was much more suitable for flying column operations.

The General Headquarters of the IRA recognised the benefit of the flying column and issued Operational Memos relating to them during September and October 1920.

Operational Order No. 1
Devolved permission to carry out attacks on military and police patrols to officers of the rank of captain.

Operational Order No. 2
Ordered Brigade commandants to closely observe enemy formations so that no opportunity to attack them would be lost.

Operational Order No. 3
Ordered the interception of all police and military communications.

Operational Order No. 4
Ordered that the worst and most vicious of the RIC were to be shot.

Operational Order No. 5
Ordered that all Black and Tans were to be shot on sight.

Operational Order No. 6
Not found.

---

33   Paddy Whelan, *WS No. 1449*, pp. 35–36.

Operational Order No. 7

1. The flying column commander must endeavour to gain experience for himself and for his men by planning and then carrying out simple operations as outlined in Operational Orders Nos 1–7.[34]
2. By harassing smaller and quieter military and police stations.
3. By intercepting and pillaging stores belonging to the enemy.
4. By intercepting communications.
5. By covering towns threatened by reprisal parties.

Following their stay at Knockraha, the members of the column moved to Shanagarry in an attempt to engage the British, but without success. From here they travelled to Ballymacoda, Ladysbridge and on to Aghada, but again failed to make contact. On 11th December 1920, they lay in ambush positions near Aghada, expecting to engage a patrol from Fort Carlisle (Fort Davis), but again the British did not appear.[35] From Aghada, they marched to billet for the night in Bertie Walsh's house in Rock Street, Cloyne. This was a dangerous move as Walsh himself was on the run, and there was a possibility that the house was being watched. The house was surrounded by British troops the following morning and it was only by guile and an aggressive break out that the column managed to escape.[36] The local Companies were rushing to their assistance after word reached them that the column was in difficulty. There were two similarities with Clonmult, in that there were no sentries in position and the house was surrounded. There was one major difference, the column members escaped from Cloyne, at Clonmult only one would escape.

The column moved from Cloyne to an unoccupied farmhouse at Kilmountain, about three miles east of Midleton, where they spent Christmas 1920. While there, word was received that a joint RIC/Black and Tan foot patrol operated on the Main Street of Midleton every night. The decision was taken by Diarmuid O'Hurley to attack the patrol on the night of 29th December. Before the attack the entire column moved into Midleton under cover of darkness and assembled in the sawmills on Charles Street. From there, the members of the column moved into their attacking positions by getting through the back gardens and yards of the houses and shops and finally coming through the houses and waiting inside the front doors until the patrol had passed on the outward leg.

---

34   U.C.D., A.D., *Organisational Memo No. 1*, p. 17b/127.
35   Paddy Whelan, *WS No. 1449*, p. 38.
36   *Rebel Corks Fighting Story*, pp. 187–188.

The eight-man foot patrol left the RIC barracks at about 9.30 pm and proceeded down Main Street. They were ambushed on the return leg as the patrol was approaching the Town Hall, now the library. During the engagement Special Constable Martin Mullen, stationed in Midleton and living with his family in Youghal, was mortally wounded. He died of his wounds that night in a house off Main Street.[37] Two Black and Tans, Ernest Dray and Arthur Thorp, were also mortally wounded.[38] The other members of the foot patrol were RIC sergeants Edward Moloney and Michael Nolan, and Black and Tans Frederick Partridge, John Gordon and Thomas Hill.[39]

During this operation, Vice-Commandant Joseph Ahern was in charge of a squad of volunteers that included Paddy Higgins and he was not impressed with Higgins's performance.[40] Ahern stated that, 'O'Higgins on that occasion didn't show any great aptitude for the work.'[41] This observation was to have serious implications in the subsequent battle at Clonmult. A mobile patrol of police on their way from Cork in response to the attack was itself ambushed at Ballyrichard near Carrigtwohill. This mobile patrol was commanded by Temporary County Inspector (T.C.I.) J.J.T. Carroll, RIC.

After this engagement the column rendezvoused at the sawmills and immediately returned to their billet at Kilmountain. Early in the New Year they moved to Griffins farmhouse at Cottstown, Dungourney.[42] From there on or about 6th January 1921, they relocated to a disused farmhouse at Garrylaurence, the scene of the Battle of Clonmult.

---

37 UK PRO, Kew, London, WO 35/155A, Military Court of Inquiry into his death, also James Herlihy, RIC historian.

38 Richard Abbott, *Police Casualties in Ireland 1919–1922*, pp. 168–169.

39 James Herlihy, RIC historian.

40 Joseph Ahern, *WS No. 1367*, p. 55.

41 *Ibid.*

42 Tomás O'Riordán, East Cork historian.

THE COLUMN'S FAILED SECURITY PLAN

The disused farmhouse at Garrylaurence was located on rising ground approximately 800 metres north-west of Clonmult village. While it was in a remote location, it could be seen from quite a distance from the eastern side. The farmhouse when it was first occupied by the column was at least adequate for their survival and offered basic living conditions. It afforded protection from the elements, and was large enough to house twenty men. There was a ready supply of water and the local population were generous with providing provisions. Use was also made of Cronin's and Bob Murray's public houses for obtaining provisions.[1]

The farmhouse was approximately 15 metres long and 5 metres wide with an outhouse at either end. The outhouse on the west side was flush with the dwelling area and had a corrugated iron roof. The outhouse on the east was connected to the dwelling area and set back approximately 2 metres and had a red-tiled roof. There were two doors on the south side or front of the main building, facing the yard. Looking from the front, the left door led into the outhouse, which was not interlinked with the accommodation area. The door on the right led into the accommodation area, the part occupied by the column.

The accommodation area consisted of three rooms on the ground floor. Immediately inside the front door was a large kitchen with an open fire, a small room or scullery to the right or east side and a parlour on the left or west of the kitchen.[2] It had three windows at the front of the accommodation area, one for each of the rooms and just one small window at the rear of the building, the window for the kitchen. At the back of the kitchen was a ladder leading to the loft in the attic space, used for sleeping. There was a dormer-type window

---

1   Patrick Whelan, *WS No. 1449*, p. 52.
2   UKNA WO 71/380, Clonmult Military Court case file, Jeremiah O'Leary's evidence.

partially built into the upper part of the east gable and the thatched roof, to provide some natural light into the loft. The roof of the accommodation area was thatched.[3] A major disadvantage for the column was the lack of a door at the rear of the accommodation area of the house. The rear wall of the house was running parallel with and approximately 3 metres from a low ditch.

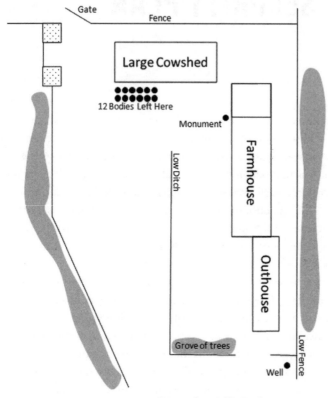

Plan of the battle site at Garrylaurence, Clonmult, 20th February 1921.

On the south side of the farmhouse there was a farmyard approximately 25 metres by 15 metres bordered on the south side by a solid ditch.[4] There was a grove of approximately twenty trees outside the yard on the eastern end, near the well. The well for fresh water was located approximately 30 metres east of

---

3   Jack O'Connell, *WS No. 1444*, p. 8.
4   *Ibid.*.

the house and is still in use today. On the western side, a large cowshed was at right angles and not connected to the farmhouse.

It appears that when Comdt O'Hurley moved his column into the building, he overlooked the design of the farmhouse and its shortcomings with regards to lack of a back door and lack of firing ports in the walls. The building needed to be both reasonably secure and also capable of being evacuated quickly even while under enemy attack.

The normal procedure in such circumstances would have been to improve the defensiveness of the house by digging, at the very least, holes between the dwelling area and the outhouses, also firing-loopholes and escape holes out through the rear wall. As Jeremiah 'Sonny' O'Leary and James Glavin found out during the battle, it was too late attempting to dig these when under fire and the house surrounded. The fact that this work was not undertaken meant that there was no way out except through the front door, and also those inside were unable to bring down maximum and effective fire on the Crown Forces due to a lack of firing positions.

The men of the flying column were billeted in the disused farmhouse at Garrylaurence, Clonmult, for about five weeks prior to the battle.[5] The fact that they were there for so long contravened the normal activities of these IRA formations and was in conflict with its title 'Flying', which conjures up images of a type of commando, i.e. lightly armed, capable of hitting its enemy anywhere and constantly on the move.

Volunteer Daniel Cashman, a full-time member of the column from its beginning and luckily on weekend leave during the battle, explained the reason for remaining so long in the one location:

> It should be recorded that the farmhouse in which we stayed was used as a headquarters for collections for the Dáil Loan which were being carried out in the surrounding districts at the time. The collectors brought the subscriptions to our billet, the monies were then checked by Diarmuid O'Hurley and sent on to a man named Cronin in the village of Clonmult. To my certain knowledge Diarmuid O'Hurley objected to the column being kept so long in Clonmult doing this work, as he maintained it was not part of their duty or his.[6]

To gain an insight into how such camps operated, one can refer to an account by Tom Barry, of a training camp for officers, held in the Third (West Cork)

---

5   *Ibid.* also Joseph Ahern, *WS No. 1367*, p. 51.
6   Daniel Cashman, *WS No. 1523*, p. 9.

Brigade area during September 1920.[7] Tom Barry was able to use his British Army training and his experiences while serving in the First World War. The norm for a training camp, which lasted a minimum of seven days, included a major emphasis on camp defence and the security measures to be enforced to avoid a surprise attack by British Forces.[8] A typical training programme provided lectures on engineering, first-aid and map reading.

The commander of any military formation is ultimately responsible for what is termed as 'terrain analyses'. Firstly, Comdt O'Hurley would have decided that the location of the training camp was suitable not only for the purpose of training but more importantly, the location had to be suitable from a security perspective. It had to be suitable for defence purposes and also to afford the opportunity to vacate the location while under fire should the situation arise. In the case of a guerrilla army, it was essential that the location be in an area where the local population was supportive of their cause.

In this instance, the location was certainly suitable for training as the terrain provided adequate facilities for conducting guerrilla-style tactical training. The buildings provided suitable cover for the theory lessons essential to educate these part-time soldiers in the art of warfare. The buildings were large enough to billet approximately twenty members and the local population was indeed supportive with adequate foodstuffs.

It is generally accepted that no terrain will provide all the essentials required for defence, so it is important that work be undertaken to improve and strengthen the defences. I have concluded that no such work was undertaken.

When carrying out terrain analysis, Comdt O'Hurley should have examined the terrain around his position, in this case the farmhouse, not just from his position from within but also from the view of an attacking force. The terrain surrounding the battle site today is quite different to what it was in 1921. Some of the ditches have been removed, but, more importantly, the wooded area north and north-west of the site extended much closer to the house. A map, surveyed about 1904, clearly shows this.[9] The wooded area is important. On inspecting the 1904 Ordnance Survey map, it can be seen that the wood came within about 200 metres of the farmhouse. Forest paths are to be seen on the map; they are running in the direction from which the British troops

7   Tom Barry, *Guerrilla Days in Ireland*, p. 19.
8   *Ibid.*
9   *Ordnance Survey Maps*, 1904, Sheet No. 54, Cork, Boole Library, U.C.C.

approached and may well have been used by them as they provided a concealed ingress route.[10]

When the column occupied the farmhouse on or about 6th January 1921, emphasis was indeed placed on security. Two sentries were posted during the day and at night two extra sentries were detailed to patrol the roads in the neighbourhood. All sentries were armed with a rifle, a revolver and a whistle with which to alert the other members in the event of danger. One of the sentries was also issued with a telescope during the day.[11] The nature of the terrain was such that the number of sentries was adequate if they were properly positioned, briefed, remained alert, irregularly inspected and remained at their posts.

Perimeter security, which was the responsibility of the sentries, was at times quite lax. Seamus Fitzgerald, T.D. in the First Dáil, Chairman of the Parish Court, Cobh and President of East Cork District Court, visited the farmhouse about one week prior to the battle.

He related:

> I proceeded to Clonmult at once, and advanced towards the farmhouse in which the column was staying. I was, of course, guided safely after making the necessary contacts en route. I had expected to be challenged by their sentries, but I was in the farmhouse before I was recognised and brought inside to meet Paddy Whelan, Paddy Sullivan, Maurice Moore and young Glavin, all from Cobh, together with the other column men from Midleton and other units. [Diarmuid O'] Hurley was expected shortly, and when he arrived he challenged me crossly for having come. He must have been displeased with the easy manner in which I had approached without being properly challenged.[12]

Comdt O'Hurley, when he analysed the surrounding terrain, looking for possible avenues of approach that the British forces might possibly use, would have seen at least five possible ingress routes.

These were:

1 From Midleton via Dungourney and directly to Clonmult village.
2. From Dungourney using the Castlelyons road via Rathorgan cross roads.

---

10   *Ibid.*
11   Joseph Ahern, *WS No. 1367*, p. 54.
12   Seamus Fitzgerald, *WS No. 1737*, p. 34.

3. From Fermoy through Castlelyons to Rathorgan cross roads.
4. From Tallow into Clonmult.
5. From Dungourney taking the upper road to Castlelyons and Fermoy or this road in reverse.

Comdt O'Hurley came to the conclusion that the threat existed only from the Dungourney to Clonmult road. His response to this threat involved the ringing of the church bell in Clonmult in the event of British forces arriving in the village and this was meant to alert the column at the farmhouse.[13] It is not stated in any of the Witness Statements whose responsibility this was. As the church was adjacent to Cronin's public house it is possible that one of the Cronin brothers, both active in the Volunteers, would carry out this task.

Comdt O'Hurley dismissed the threat from the upper road because he believed that this was considered by the British as too dangerous to travel on.[14] This is an unusual deduction, as I have not found any record of an attack on British forces in the area either prior to or subsequent to the battle of Clonmult. When troops are in a fixed position, as the column was in this case, it is fundamental that preparations are made to repulse the enemy from any direction they may attack from. Tactical drills need to be rehearsed so that reaction to attack is immediate, greatly increasing the chance of a successful outcome.

The defence and security of the column within the immediate vicinity of the farmhouse was the responsibility of the column itself. On occasions when a flying column was billeted in an area for a short stay, the local Volunteer Company usually provided sentries, thus enabling all members of the column to sleep securely. As was the case at Clonmult, when the column was billeted in the area for a considerable period, the sentries were detailed from the column members. However, part of the security plan involved the local Volunteer Company coming to the assistance of the column should the need arise.[15]

To quote Vice-Commandant J. Ahern:

When the column entered a company area instructions were issued that if the column happened to be surrounded, the local company or companies were to mobilise all available men and come to their aid. In Cloyne when the column was surrounded in Bertie Walsh's house on 12th of Dec., 1920, these arrangements worked well as Ladysbridge and Cloyne and portion of the

---

13   Jack O'Connell, *WS No. 1444*, p. 14.
14   *Ibid.*
15   Joseph Ahern, *WS No. 1367*, p. 52.

Aghada Companies were actually converging on Cloyne when the column fought their way out.[16]

On the Sunday afternoon when the column did find itself trapped, no assistance was forthcoming from the local Company. I emphasise Sunday because it would be expected that the local members would have been at home and thus in a position to render assistance. Considering the lack of strength of the assaulting force of British troops, it is conceivable that a little fire support from the local Volunteers could have made the difference.

Comdt O'Hurley was in a predicament, because, while on the one hand he had to plan for a situation where the column may be trapped in the house, at the same time he would have known that his priority would be to escape entrapment, as had almost occurred at Bertie Walsh's house in Cloyne, on Sunday morning on 12th December.

To quote Capt Paddy Whelan: 'If enemy troops arrived, it was anticipated that their presence would become known to us in advance, and I know it was Diarmuid O'Hurley's intention, in such circumstances, to evacuate the building and give battle outside.'[17]

The time spent at Clonmult was used to give the members of the column an opportunity for some concentrated training and specifically to plan and prepare for a second attack on Castlemartyr RIC Barracks. This barracks had been captured previously, but, due to it being located between two dwelling houses the IRA decided not to destroy it. The training would have included lessons on military tactics, signalling, first-aid and the use of explosives. As all members of the column had battle experience, shooting practice was deemed unnecessary. During this time there was a constant turnover of men, because as some returned to their home Company locations they were replaced by other men. Cobh men, Jack O'Connell and James Ahern, joined the column exactly one week before the battle.[18] Pat O'Sullivan and Maurice Moore joined the column during the two weeks prior to the battle.

While the column was based in the farmhouse, it is very important to bear in mind that they were still possibly at the top of the Crown Forces most wanted list in East Cork and Cork City. The RIC in Midleton and the 17th Infantry Brigade Intelligence Branch in Victoria Barracks were actively working to locate and neutralise the unit. The attack on the foot patrol in Midleton on

---

16   Joseph Ahern, *WS No. 1367*, p. 55.
17   Patrick Whelan, *WS No. 1449*, p. 50.
18   Seamus Fitzgerald, TD, *WS No. 1737*, pp. 34–35.

29th December resulting in the killing of the three RIC constables would only have increased their efforts. Overt patrolling and covert methods such as using spies and informers and the interrogation of prisoners would all have been used extensively in their attempt to gather information and to locate the column.

A major effort on the part of the column and the column commander would have been required at all times to maintain security of their location. Keeping between fifteen and twenty men of the column for so long in the one place was really asking for trouble. While the farmhouse was remote it was never-theless within 800 metres of the local Catholic Church and a school, both places of public assembly. In addition, having to arrange the feeding of so many men for so long would definitely have increased the number of locals aware of the column's location and put a strain on the resources of the local farming community. It is also believed that while in Clonmult members of the column participated in dances in local houses. We also know that during their time in other locations photographs were taken of individual members and groups of the column. All of these factors greatly affected the security of the column. Eventually the Crown Forces would get the information they needed.

The men were finalising their planned attack on Castlemartyr RIC Barracks when a dispatch was received from the Adjutant of the 1st Brigade, Maj Florrie O'Donoghue, instructing them to attack a military train at Cobh Junction. This was the junction of the Cobh to Cork and Midleton to Cork railway lines. The dispatch ended with the words, 'if you are unable to carry out the job, please let me know immediately and I will make other arrange-ments'. The suggestion that the column may not be capable of undertaking this mission greatly annoyed the officers who read it. Previous assistance from the 1st Brigade had been very limited, further fuelling their anger. 'The only help we received from the brigade during the whole period was a gift of 48 lbs. of gelignite and a small exploder.'[19]

The last few days were spent preparing for the move out. Arrangements were made for the column to be billeted at Dooneen, near Leamlara on Sunday night, 20th February. On Friday, 18th February, the IRA entered the house of P.H. Barry, at Ballyadam, near Carrigtwohill. They removed beds, bedding, delph, jewellery and £7 in cash.[20] The owner was opposed to the IRA and had refused to subscribe to its upkeep. This house was only a few miles from

19   Joseph Ahern, *WS No. 1367*, p. 51.
20   British in Ireland, Reel No. 74, Jan–March 1921, *RIC County Inspector's Monthly Confidential Report, February 1921*, CO 904/114, Boole Library, U.C.C.

Dooneen and it is possible that the items were required to furnish the new billet for the column.

On Saturday, 19th February, the day before the battle, some of the column members went to Dungourney for confession. Jack O'Connell stated that this was when the informer, an ex-soldier out trapping rabbits, observed the volunteers returning from Dungourney.[21] As a precaution the column men were using the less direct Dungourney–Castlelyons road, rather than going through Clonmult village. They used this road as far as Carey's house and then used paths through the wood to get to the farmhouse. This led the informer to conclude that the column was based in Carey's house. The Crown Forces were indeed working hard and using all their resources to locate the column.

Capt William Buckley, an officer with the Conna flying column, recalled:

> While on our way with O'Malley, I noticed a man washing his socks in the river at the bridge south of Glenville. As the enemy were at this time sending members of their forces, dressed in civilian clothes, into the area to act as spies, I became suspicious of this individual. Early next morning the area was surrounded by enemy troops.[22]

On Sunday morning, 20th February, Dick Hegarty was at home at Moanroe, Garryvoe, just finishing a few days' leave from the column. He was taken to Clonmult in a ginnet and trap, driven by his uncle, Michael Kennefick, and accompanied by his brother, Jack.[23] After dropping Dick off in Clonmult village at about 2 pm, the two men while on their way home saw two truckloads of Auxiliary Police in Castlemartyr. There is a good possibility that these were the same Auxiliaries that reinforced the British troops in Clonmult later that evening.[24]

John Harty and his friend, Edmond Terry, who were both members of Na Fianna, the IRA youth organisation, met in Churchtown South after mass on the morning of the battle. It had been arranged that they would take funds that had been collected from the farmers in their area to the column headquarters, which was a collecting point for such monies. This money was levied on farmers and used as a war chest by the IRA. It was also arranged that they would bring cigarettes and clean laundry for the IRA men. On their way to Clonmult,

---

21 Jack O'Connell, *WS No. 1444*, p. 13.
22 William Buckley, *WS No. 1009*, p. 21.
23 Extract from a letter written by a sister of Dick Hegarty, Hegarty family archives.
24 Letter in Hegarty family archives.

they met two of their friends in Ladysbridge, Robert Walsh of Ballycotton and William Garde, Shanagarry, who may not have been members of Na Fianna.[25] The four cycled to Clonmult village, arriving there just before Dick Hegarty. The four stopped at the crossroads in Clonmult village and Edmond Terry took the opportunity to visit his grandmother, Mrs Fitzgerald. While the other three were waiting outside, Dick Hegarty arrived. They waited for Edmond Terry and the five set off for the farmhouse, approximately 2 kilometres away.

---

25   *Cork Examiner,* Wednesday, 15th March 1921.

THE COLUMN'S RECONNAISSANCE GROUP

Having received his mission from 1st Brigade Headquarters in Cork City to carry out an attack on a train conveying explosives and soldiers of the Cameron Highlanders from Cobh to Cork on the following Tuesday, 22nd February, the column commander had to carry out a reconnaissance of the area of Cobh Junction, where the attack was to take place.[1] This was to familiarise himself with the terrain in order for him to plan the ambush and to decide on the disposition of his men. This reconnaissance would enable him to formulate a plan and to then brief those involved in the ambush.

The composition and activities of the reconnaissance group that departed the farmhouse at Clonmult, sometime between 2 and 3 pm on that Sunday afternoon, deserves careful analysis.[2] Previous accounts have given different timings, even different dates for the departure from Clonmult, but the details here are now confirmed from the Witness Statements.

The initial reconnaissance group consisted of the Column Commander, Comdt O'Hurley, and his second-in-command, Vice-Comdt Joseph Ahern. Capt Paddy Whelan was to be left in charge of the column, being the next senior officer. However, neither of the two officers was familiar with the area around Cobh Junction, therefore, Paddy Whelan, who was familiar with the terrain, was included in the reconnaissance group at short notice.[3]

When they were leaving, Capt Jack O'Connell of Cobh was appointed as acting Column Commander over the head of Capt Paddy Higgins, who was senior to Capt O'Connell. This led to friction between the two officers and a conflict of command. Capt O'Connell was ordered by Comdt O'Hurley to

---

1   Joseph Ahern, *WS No. 1367*, p. 51, and Patrick Whelan, *WS No. 1449*, p. 50.
2   Patrick Whelan, *WS No. 1449*, p. 52.
3   *Ibid*. p. 51.

vacate the farmhouse at 6 o'clock that evening and march the column approximately six miles to the west to their new billets at Dooneen, Leamlara.

The reconnaissance group left the area in a Ford car. When they had driven down to the T-junction, where they could have turned left in the direction of Clonmult Church, a debate started between O'Hurley and Ahern about going up to Bob Murray's public house in Clonmult to thank him for his hospitality, now that they were leaving the area for some time.[4] The reason they decided against going up there was they could not afford the time delay that would result from further hospitality, which was almost certain to be extended by the publican. Had they decided to go to Murray's, it would have meant that they would be still in the area when the attack on the farmhouse commenced. Having these three men in the area, but outside the British Army cordon around the farmhouse, could have made all the difference to the outcome of the battle. However, this was not to be; they drove through Rathorgan Crossroads and on to Cobh Junction, which was about fourteen miles to the south.

I now wish to examine the composition of the reconnaissance group. The reconnaissance party consisted of the three most senior officers of the column. The normal military procedure was that the commander carried out the reconnaissance, accompanied by any advisors he may have required, in this instance Capt Paddy Whelan because of his familiarity with Cobh Junction. In addition, he should bring along some riflemen as security, and a driver. While the Column Commander was carrying out his reconnaissance his second-in-command, Vice-Comdt Joseph Ahern, should have been left in charge of the column. By taking so many senior officers along, the column was being stripped of its leadership.

The duty of the second-in-command in this situation was that he would assume the temporary responsibility of command. He would move the column at the designated time to the location of the rendezvous, as instructed by Comdt O'Hurley. The order was to vacate the farmhouse at 6 pm and march to new billets at Dooneen, near Leamlara.[5] Here, the reconnaissance party and the remainder of the column would be reunited. With Comdt O'Hurley back in command, Vice-Comdt Ahern would resume his duties as second-in-command. Comdt O'Hurley would then prepare his battle plan based on his reconnaissance and his resources, and issue his orders to the column.

The decision to appoint Capt Jack O'Connell as acting Column Commander over Capt Paddy Higgins was divisive within the column. The decision to over-

---

4   Patrick Whelan, *WS No. 1449*, p. 52.
5   *Ibid.*

look Capt Paddy Higgins as acting Column Commander appears to have had its origins as far back as 29th December, when the column attacked the joint RIC/Black and Tan foot patrol on the Main Street of Midleton. Paddy Higgins was with Joseph Ahern's group and he was not impressed by Higgins' lack of effort during the gun battle that left two Black and Tans and an RIC constable dead. Ahern says, 'Higgins on that occasion didn't show any great aptitude for the work, so I decided to pass him over on this occasion.'[6] This is the reason Ahern gives for O'Connell being appointed as acting officer commanding the column over Higgins.[7] It was therefore a weakened and divided column that found itself surrounded in the farmhouse at Clonmult.

---

6   Joseph Ahern, *WS No. 1367*, p. 55.
7   *Ibid*.

THE BRITISH ARMY AT CLONMULT

The concerted effort and perseverance of the Crown Forces in their search for the column was making progress. 'For some days in the middle of February, a good deal of valuable information regarding the movements and personnel of a flying column in the Clonmult area was being obtained by the intelligence officer of the 2nd Battalion of the Hampshire Regiment in Victoria Barracks, detailed information regarding the position of this column was obtained and promptly acted upon.'[1]

Col C. French, Commanding Officer of the 2nd Battalion, Hampshire Regiment, reported: 'I allowed these operations (Clonmult) to be carried out by the troops in the Cork area in order to save time and because the information on which they were based was obtained in Cork.'[2]

At about midday on Sunday, February 20th information was received at Victoria Barracks to the effect that a much wanted rebel and his 'Active Service Unit' were living in a farmhouse in the neighbourhood of Clonmult, a remote village in the East of the County of Cork. It was decided to endeavour to round up this party at once, as 'Active Service Units' seldom stay more than once in the same place, and a day lost might mean a fruitless search. At two o'clock that afternoon, a party of four officers and twenty other ranks left Cork for Clonmult, via Midleton RIC Barracks.[3]

---

1   The Irish Rebellion in the 6th Division Area, Imperial War Museum, London, EPS/2/2, also *The Irish Sword*, Spring 2010, No. 107, p. 84.
2   Clonmult report by Col C. French, Commanding Officer, 2nd Battalion, The Hampshire Regt, also see Appendix 13.
3   British Army report reprinted in *An tOglach*, 7th October 1921, p. 2, Irish Military Archives.

Having set up their patrol harbour at Rathorgan Cross Roads and having set off, the report continued:

> This involved a lot of crawling and creeping under cover of the banks and hedges, a slow performance but a necessary one, owing to the fact that the 'Shinner' is usually a very wide awake person. Eventually the house was surrounded and rushed, fortunately in silence as it proved to be the wrong house.[4]

The British Army mobile patrol that arrived at Clonmult had departed Victoria Barracks in Cork City at 2.15 pm on Sunday, 20th February.[5] Based on what was considered as good intelligence received, the mobile patrol commander, Lt D.F. Hook, M.C., 2nd Battalion, Hampshire Regiment, had been tasked with conducting a cordon and search of a house in the Clonmult area in order to locate and destroy the column. The strength of the British Army at Clonmult has been estimated in previous accounts of the battle as being up to Company strength, which would number approximately 120 men.[6] It would have required eleven Crossley tenders to transport such a force. *The Regimental History of the Royal Hampshire Regiment* gives the strength of the patrol as four officers and twenty-one other ranks (soldiers) from the Regiment.[7] Two Crossley tenders were used to transport this force and were driven by two Royal Army Service Corps (RASC) drivers, giving a total of twenty-seven personnel. This number plus the informer, also taken to Clonmult, both as a guide and hostage, corresponds with the carrying capacity of two Crossley tenders, which was fourteen personnel per vehicle including the driver. Local civilians that went to Rathorgan Crossroads, where the British parked the vehicles, reported later that there were indeed two Crossley tenders parked there.[8] The civilians were also warned not to approach one of the tenders. The belief later was that the informer was on board.

There were three officers on the patrol from the 2nd Battalion, Hampshire Regiment: the patrol commander Lt D.F. Hook, M.C., Lt A.R. Koe, Lt G.R.A. Dove, along with Lt H. Hammond, M.C., intelligence officer of the

---

4   *Ibid.*
5   See Appendix 12, (1).
6   *Rebel Cork's Fighting Story*, p. 191, see also, John McCann, 'Thirty Pieces of Silver', in, *War by the Irish*, p. 153.
7   David Scott Daniel, *The Regimental History of the Royal Hampshire Regiment*, Vol. 3, p. 10.
8   Michael Hennessy, in, Tony Moore's, Clonmult and the Construction of Legend, University of Humberside, B.A. Thesis, 1996, p. 11.

17th Infantry Brigade.[9] The senior N.C.O. was Company Sgt Maj Edward Corney, M.M. Lt Dove was also an intelligence officer of the Cork City Intelligence Office.[10]

The mobile patrol departed Victoria barracks in Cork City at 2.15 pm, under the overall command of Lt Hook.[11] The patrol drove directly to the Royal Irish Constabulary Barracks, in Midleton. The RIC barracks, subsequently the old Gárda station, stood on the courthouse side of the present Gárda station. This was standard procedure to inform the local RIC officer that the army patrol was operating in the vicinity and to tell them of their mission and their destination. From Midleton, the mobile patrol travelled north on the Lisgoold–Fermoy road for approximately one mile, where it turned right, past where the East Cork Oil depot is presently situated. The patrol continued north, passing through Elfordstown, taking the right fork beyond where the Earth Station is located. From here it continued on to the Dispensary Crossroads, it turned right and travelled directly to Rathorgan Crossroads. The total distance from Midleton is approximately ten miles.

When the mobile patrol arrived at Rathorgan Crossroads at approximately 3 pm, it was decided to leave the two tenders there and use the crossroads as a patrol harbour. One of the Crossley tenders was parked on the other side of the junction facing Dungourney. The other was parked facing down the road the troops had arrived from. This location was ideal for parking the two tenders as any attempt to drive the vehicles nearer to where they believed the column was located would have increased the chances of the element of surprise being lost. The location was also used to detain two local men who happened to walk to the crossroads.

The patrol was now broken down into three groups. The first group consisted of one N.C.O., six soldiers and the two drivers; these were left to guard the vehicles, the informer and to detain any civilians.[12] This group had another very important purpose: in the event of the attacking force meeting overwhelming opposition, they would have been able to withdraw back to the crossroads under covering fire from the soldiers located there. The second group was the foot patrol with Lt A.R. Koe in charge and included Lt H. Hammond, CSM Corney, and seven soldiers. The third group was another

---

9   N.L.I., *O'Donoghue Papers*, MS 31223 (1).
10   UKNA, Kew, London, Clonmult file WO 71/380.
11   WO 71/380, Lt Koe's evidence.
12   *Regimental History of the Royal Hampshire Regiment*, Vol. 3, pp. 9–11.

foot patrol with Lt Hook in charge, with Lt Dove and six soldiers. The two foot patrols made up the attacking force and were now ready to move out.

From the actions of the two foot patrols, it is now conclusive that the mobile patrol was acting on information received. However, the informer had come to an incorrect conclusion as to the exact location of the column. He had concluded that they were in Carey's dwelling house. Also, it can be concluded from the strength of the patrol, or lack of it, that the troops were only expecting to find possibly five or six Volunteers, a squad and not a full column. This also ties in with the number that went to Dungourney for confession on the Saturday evening. The informer had spotted the members of the column on their return journey to the farmhouse and could only follow them as far as Carey's house. The volunteers had taken the Dungourney–Rathorgan Cross Roads–Castlelyons road as far as Carey's house. Using what is still considered an essential precaution, they then continued to the farmhouse using the less obvious and more covert route through the forest.

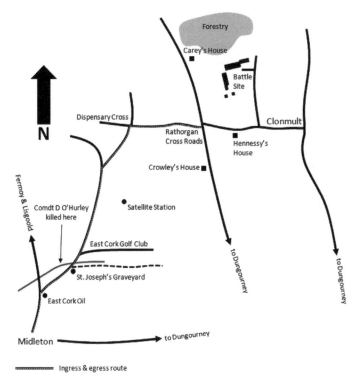

Ingress and egress route taken by Crown Forces from Midleton to Rathorgan crossroads, 20th February 1921.

Departing Rathorgan Crossroads, the patrols set off on their mission, to carry out a cordon and search of their objective, the home of the Carey family, located approximately 400 metres north of the crossroads. The two foot patrols advanced approximately 100 metres west, on the public road they had driven on. They then advanced north across the fields, on the western side of a ditch. By keeping the ditch on their right or eastern side, they were hidden from view, thus preventing anyone in Carey's house from observing them. They used the ditch lines to maximum effect and this brought the troops very close to the western side of Carey's house. The patrols advanced cautiously on this cottage because they had concluded from intelligence reports that this was where the column was billeted. This cottage was searched without result. 'Eventually the house was surrounded and rushed, unfortunately in silence, as it proved to be the wrong house'.[13] The officers, after consulting their map, decided to search another house 350 metres to the east. This house was south-east of Garrylaurence Wood.[14] This time there was no mistake.

The reason that the two British Army foot patrols were able to reach the farmhouse where the column was billeted maintaining the element of surprise was because the two IRA sentries had abandoned their posts without being properly relieved. Both were in the farmhouse packing their belongings for the march out after dusk.[15] There was going to be no early warning for the men inside. Capt Paddy Higgins later recalled: 'regarding the security arrangements during this period, I understood that the local Company would do sentry duty etc., why they did not do so or what went wrong I do not know'.[16] In reality, the responsibility for perimeter security was the column's until and unless properly relieved.

---

13   British Army report reprinted in *An tOglach, 7th October 1921*, p. 2,
      Irish Military Archives.
14   Lt. A.R. Koe's after action report, see Appendix 12, (4).
15   Jack O'Connell, *WS No. 1444*, p. 14.
16   P.J. Higgins lecture, *The Story of Clonmult*, 1971, p. 4, NLI, MS 44,047/3,
      O'Mahony Papers.

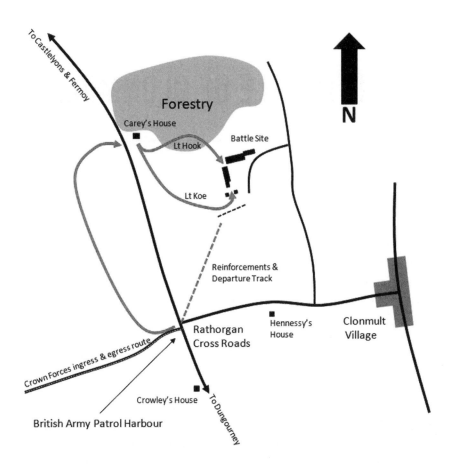

Map of the Clonmult district, 20th February 1921.

THE BATTLE OF CLONMULT

When Dick Hegarty and the four cyclists, William Garde, John Harty, Robert Walsh and Edmond Terry, arrived at the farmhouse on the Sunday afternoon they brought the total in the farmhouse to twenty-one. As they arrived they met John Joe Joyce and Michael Desmond; both men were walking to the well to collect water to make tea prior to the march out.[1] The well was approximately 30 metres east of the house and is still in use today. The time was approximately 4 pm. The time was also confirmed by Jack O'Connell.

Dick Hegarty and the four cyclists had just reached the farmyard when they heard a shout to get inside the house to safety. Jeremiah (Diarmuid) O'Leary was looking out one of the windows and suddenly spotted the British soldiers: 'I chanced to look out a front window and saw, to my amazement, soldiers crawling past the gateway near the lane. I immediately gave the alarm and, almost at once, the military opened fire on us from all sides.'[2]

The five ran into the house and the four young cyclists spent the next two hours lying on the floor of the kitchen and under the table while the shooting went on around them.[3] This was the beginning of the most traumatic and terrifying experience of their lives.

Unknown to those inside, only the patrol under Lt Koe had reached the farmhouse. Lt Koe, Lt Hammond, CSM Corney and seven soldiers had approached from the south-west. Lt Koe detailed six soldiers to line the ditch on the western side of the main building.[4] Lt Koe, on seeing the number of

1   *Cork Examiner*, Wednesday, 16th March 1921.
2   Diarmuid (Jeremiah) O'Leary, *WS No. 1589*, p. 5.
3   UKNA, Kew, Clonmult file WO 71/380, John Harty defence evidence.
4   UKNA Kew, WO 71/380, Clonmult case file, Lt A.R. Koe's evidence, pp. 36–40.

bicycles that were against the wall of the farmhouse, knew that at that stage it was the British military that were outnumbered. It was this patrol that made the first contact.

This was the same time that Michael Desmond and John Joe Joyce were going to the well to collect water for the column. The two volunteers became engaged in a very brief gun battle with the British soldiers belonging to Lt Koe's patrol as they were manoeuvring to surround the house. The two IRA men were each armed with revolvers, one also had a rifle with a fixed bayonet, while the other had a double-barrelled shotgun. Both were outgunned as well as being outnumbered by the British troops. This one-sided engagement was quickly over with both IRA men mortally wounded. Before he died, John Joe Joyce managed to crawl to the window at the rear of the house and call out to those inside that the house was surrounded.[5] Desmond and Joyce died at the rear or north side of the house. Joyce died so near to the house that his body was partially burned by the burning thatch falling from the roof.

While this initial engagement was taking place, two local men, Michael Hennessy and John Crowley, were finishing dinner in the Hennessy house, located east of the crossroads on the road to Clonmult village. Crowley's house was just south of the crossroads, on the Dungourney road. Afterwards, around 3.30 p.m. the two men were walking towards the crossroads when they heard noise from the direction of the farmhouse where the column was located. The men concluded that the noise they heard, which was the gunfire of the opening shots of the battle, sounded like someone breaking timber. The comment was, 'why are they breaking timber and they are leaving tonight?' Even the locals knew the column's departure plans.

The two men walked towards the crossroads, along a track that ran parallel to the public road. Approaching the crossroads, a shout rang out, 'Halt, take your hands out of your pockets and put them up.' The two men had been under observation from one of the British soldiers guarding the tenders. They were immediately taken under escort to where the remainder of the troops were located. Looking around, the two men quickly concluded that there was something suspicious about the tender in that it had its canvas cover tied down. Attempting to see who or what was inside, one of the soldiers warned them that if they came any closer they were liable to be shot

---

5   Lochlinn McGlynn and Ray Ryan, *The Kerryman*, Saturday, 20th February 1965, p. 9.

by a stray bullet. They heeded the warning. Definitely, the informer was on board under the canvas.

Meanwhile, the second patrol under Lt Hook was approximately 250 metres away from the farmhouse when the shooting started. Lt Dove, who was on that patrol with Lt Hook, stated:

> We approached the house from the west. When we were about 300 yards away I heard shots. The house was not then in sight. We at once ran in the direction of the farm and got to a bank about 100 yards from it when I saw four soldiers of the second party. On getting to within 30 yards of the house, I saw the bodies of two dead civilians at the rear of the house.[6]

The Volunteers were now in the worst possible predicament. They had been taken by surprise because their two sentries had abandoned their posts.[7] Their ability to return effective fire on the British was greatly reduced owing to a lack of firing positions, which should have been constructed during their long stay in the location. The lack of at least one other exit was now a major handicap. A secondary exit should have been knocked out of the rear wall during their period of occupation. A crawl hole would have sufficed. The only course of action open to the trapped column was an aggressive break out and this would have to be attempted before the British troops established their positions. Almost immediately, Capt Jack O'Connell, the officer in charge, assessed the situation and came to the conclusion that the prospects of fighting a winning battle from within the house were absolutely hopeless and immediately decided on attempting a break out.[8] However, a command conflict became apparent between him and Capt Paddy Higgins, who was still annoyed at being passed over by Jack O'Connell and was not inclined to charge out of the house against the British rifles. This was when the absence of the real second-in-command was to cost the column dearly. It was time for quick decisions, clear orders and instant obedience. It was not the occasion for disagreement between the two senior officers present.

The result was that only four men agreed to make an attempted break out with Capt O'Connell. These were Vol Michael Hallahan of Midleton, Capt James Ahern of Cobh, Capt Dick Hegarty of Garryvoe and Capt Jeremiah (Diarmuid) O'Leary of Killeagh. Within minutes of the first shots being fired,

---

6   UKNA, WO 71/380, Lt Dove's evidence.
7   Jack O'Connell, *WS No. 1444*, p. 14.
8   Jack O'Connell, *WS No. 1444*, p. 10.

Capt O'Connell distributed the reserve ammunition and some grenades among his men.[9] Firing was now intensified from the house, in order to provide covering fire for the men who were about to attempt to break out. With only three windows and one door at the front of the building, the lack of firing ports and a restricted field of fire greatly reduced the ability of the men remaining inside to give accurate and effective support to the five attempting the break out.

Capt O'Connell, armed with a rifle and fixed bayonet, led the break out through the door and seemingly caught the British troops by surprise.[10] He ran across the farmyard to a gateway. As he turned up to the right, he was fired on by two British soldiers from the corner of a field bordering the western side of the yard. He returned fire, wounding CSM Corney.[11] Lt Koe would later give evidence that the bullet that wounded the CSM was fired from the grove of trees. Capt O'Connell ran further down the track and when he looked around to see his companions, to his amazement he was alone. Lt Koe's account is that he, the CSM and one soldier proceeded to the eastern side of the farmhouse where there was a small wood. As they approached the eastern side of the house, fire was opened on them from near the small wood, wounding the CSM. Lt Koe and the soldier returned fire and withdrew with the wounded CSM.[12] Lt Koe and CSM Corney had been carrying out a preliminary reconnaissance of the farmhouse and yard when Capt O'Connell made his dash for freedom.

After hearing the opening shots of the first contact resulting in the deaths of the two volunteers, Lt Hook doubled forward his patrol that were approaching from the west and was just after linking up with the other patrol at the western side of the farmyard when the four volunteers dashed from the house.[13] This means that the decision and action to break out was taken within a matter of less than ten minutes from the first shots being fired.

Vol Michael Hallahan had followed Capt O'Connell and he was shot dead immediately outside the door. Capt Ahern followed next and attempted to make his escape running in a south-westerly direction, unfortunately for him, in the direction of the crossroads. He covered approximately 300 metres before being shot dead while climbing over a ditch in one of the fields. The two men detained earlier, Michael Hennessy and John Crowley, heard

---

9   *Ibid.*

10   *Ibid.*

11   *Ibid.*

12   UKNA, WO 71/380, Lt A.R. Koe's evidence, pp. 36–40.

13   UKNA WO 71/380, Lt D.F. Hook's evidence.

the shooting and concluded that James Ahern was shot dead by one of the sentries located east of the crossroads. Capt Hegarty was next out, but was shot down, mortally wounded, while attempting to reach the fence in front of the house. The last man out was Capt O'Leary:[14] 'I got into the farmyard, but, seeing the other boys fall, decided there was no hope of escape and dashed back again into the house amidst a hail of bullets, none of which, fortunately hit me.'

The dying Capt Hegarty was still managing to fire his rifle and this may have distracted the troops enough for Capt O'Leary to get back into the house.[15] The attempted break out was over. Of the five, three were dead and only one managed to get through the British Army cordon.

The British officer in command, Lt Hook, at this stage assessed the situation from his perspective and concluded that while the IRA column was trapped, he himself did not have an adequate force with which to storm and overwhelm the farmhouse in a frontal assault. He must also have been concerned that they were liable to be attacked by IRA forces outside the cordon. His plan was to maintain the cordon around the house. He decided to send two soldiers, Pte C. Sherry and one other, back to the crossroads to order one of the RASC drivers to take them to Midleton in search of bombs and reinforcements.[16] Capt O'Connell, who had survived the break out, saw the two soldiers crossing the fields in the direction of the crossroads. He fired on them but they did not return fire as their mission was to get to Midleton.

Inside the house, Capt Higgins was now in charge of a greatly reduced column. Three of the senior officers were gone on a reconnaissance, five of their comrades had been killed during the previous thirty minutes and at that stage some were convinced that Jack O'Connell may also be dead or captured, and they themselves were still surrounded. Capt Higgins decided to continue the fight from inside, hoping that some help might reach them. An element of the column's security plan was that the members of the local Volunteer Company would come to their assistance in the event of the British forces attacking them. Unfortunately, for the column, no assistance appeared to be forthcoming. They were on their own

An attempt was now made to breach one of the walls of the house. Paddy Higgins says that it was a gable wall, while Jeremiah O'Leary says it was the rear wall. As neither gable was accessible it was more than likely the rear

---

14   Diarmuid (Jeremiah) O'Leary, *WS No. 1589*, p. 6.
15   Joseph Ahern, *WS No. 1367*, p. 56.
16   UKNA WO 71/380, Lt A.R. Koe's and Pte Sherry's evidence.

wall. Bayonets, knives and forks were used to remove the stones, etc. and eventually a hole was opened large enough for a man to crawl through.[17] O'Leary was the first to attempt to get through, but, as soon as he put his head through the opening he was spotted by one of the British soldiers, who fired at him. He received a bullet wound in the head and had to be pulled back inside by his comrades. He soon lapsed into unconsciousness as a result of his wound.

When the British soldiers that were sent to Midleton for reinforcements arrived there, they found two truckloads of Auxiliary Police that were travelling between Youghal and Cork were at the RIC barracks. A number of accounts mention two truckloads of Black and Tans as being the reinforcements. The term 'Black and Tan' was used to describe and indicate both groups of ex-British military veterans recruited during 1920 to reinforce the Royal Irish Constabulary.[18] The first group arrived in March 1920 and was made up of men that were formerly enlisted ranks of the British Forces. They were officially referred to as Temporary Constables of the RIC, and were the original Black and Tans, because they initially wore a mix of British Army khaki and RIC bottle green uniforms. Within a few months they were issued with complete RIC uniforms. Around August of 1920 the Temporary Cadets of the Auxiliary Division, Royal Irish Constabulary (ADRIC), began to arrive in Ireland and again, because of their khaki and green uniforms, were also referred to as Black and Tans.[19] These men were formerly commissioned officers of the British Forces. Both groups had extensive service during the First World War.

On this occasion, it was members of the Auxiliary Division that provided the reinforcements for the British Army at Clonmult.[20] It was also standard procedure that all British military and police convoys would consist of at least two vehicles. Approximately twenty-four Auxiliaries travelled to Clonmult under the command of an RIC County Inspector.[21] When reinforcements were sought, it is my conclusion that some regular RIC and Temporary Constables from Midleton also travelled to the battle scene, including RIC Constables Henry Harris and A.B.D. Smith.[22]

---

17   Diarmuid (Jeremiah) O'Leary, *WS No. 1589*, p. 7.
18   *Irish Bulletin*, Vol. 3, 2015 reprint, Belfast Historical and Educational Society, p. 1304.
19   *Ibid*.
20   UKNA WO 71/380, Lt Dove's evidence, p. 8.
21   See Lt A R Koe's after action report, Appendix 12, (12).
22   UKNA WO 71/380, Clonmult file. Both constables were attached to Cornmarket Street RIC Barracks in Cork City.

On several occasions during the battle, the British had called on the besieged men to surrender. The IRA men were not going to give themselves up as their future prospects would have been very bleak. Just about nine weeks previously, on 11th December 1920, as a result of the Kilmichael ambush, the British authorities had declared Martial Law in the counties of Cork, Kerry, Limerick and Tipperary.[23] As a coincidence, the first official reprisals under Martial Law were carried out in Midleton.[24] It was also decreed that: 'Any unauthorised person found in possession of arms, ammunition or explosives would on conviction of a Military Court, suffer death.'

On 1st February, just three weeks prior to Clonmult, Capt Con Murphy from Millstreet was executed in Cork Military Detention Barracks after being found in possession of a revolver. This was the likely fate awaiting the besieged men.

The Crossley tenders carrying the twenty-four Auxiliary Police reinforcements, under the command of an RIC County Inspector, arrived at the Rathorgan Crossroads and parked there. The Auxiliaries then proceeded across the fields on foot and arrived at the farmhouse at about 5.20 pm.[25] The Auxiliaries were positioned on the western side of the house and at the end of the cowshed.[26] They had brought petrol and grenades with them and without delay, an army officer, Lt H. Hammond, proceeded to set fire to the thatch roof on the northern side or rear of the farmhouse using the petrol. Lt H. Hammond was the Intelligence Officer of the 17th Infantry Brigade.[27] After the fire had burned a hole in the thatch the military threw grenades into the house through the hole. The grenades had little or no effect on the trapped men as the thatch and the floorboards of the loft took the brunt of the explosives. When the sound and smell of the burning thatch reached the IRA men they knew that this was the beginning of the end. Jeremiah O'Leary recalled, 'We were getting sick from inhaling the fumes.' A British Army officer was contacted and promised that their lives would be saved if the remainder of the column surrendered.[28] This promise was highlighted later during their trial.

The decision was taken to surrender approximately fifteen minutes after the roof was set on fire. Capt Paddy Higgins ordered the men to throw their

23   Michael Hopkinson, *The Irish War of Independence*, p. 92.
24   *Ibid.* p. 93.
25   Paddy Higgins, *WS No. 1467*, also, WO 71/380, Lt Koe's evidence.
26   *Cork Examiner*, 9th March 1921, also, WO 71/380, Lt Dove's evidence.
27   UKNA, WO 71/380, Clonmult Military Court file.
28   Joseph Ahern, *WS No. 1367*, p. 57.

weapons into the fire prior to surrendering.[29] Following this, twelve men came out of the house to surrender and three were delayed behind. We know from the Military Court records that an unidentified member of the column was first out, William Garde was second, John Harty was third and Robert Walsh was fourth, followed by eight other members of the column including Paddy Higgins. John Harty was felled by being clubbed on the side of his head with the brass-plated butt of an Auxiliary's rifle. The others were lined up along the east wall of the cowshed with their hands up. Immediately the Auxiliaries opened fire and killed seven of their twelve prisoners. Lt Christopher O'Sullivan, Volunteers David Desmond, Jeremiah Ahern and his first cousin Liam Ahern, Donal Dennehy, Joseph Morrissey and James Glavin were all shot dead. Capt Higgins recalled 'a Tan put his revolver to my mouth and fired, I felt as if I was falling through a bottomless pit. Then I thought I heard a voice saying, "This fellow is not dead, we will finish him off". Only for a military officer coming along, I too would be gone.'[30] The arrival of the British Army officer ended the Auxiliaries' killing spree.

Amazingly the four young cyclists, John Harty, William Garde, Edmond Terry and Robert Walsh, all survived the killing spree, even though the first three were wounded. While their age cannot be the only reason they were not killed, because James Glavin was younger, my belief is that a contributory factor was that they were dressed entirely in civilian attire, whereas the others as members of the column would have been wearing items of military dress. Something like wearing high boots, leggings or a military belt may have sealed their fate.

Luckily for Maurice Moore and Patrick O'Sullivan, they were delayed in exiting the house as they were attempting to carry the wounded and semi-conscious Jeremiah O'Leary out and this delay saved their lives. They came out after the British officer had regained control. These three were ordered into the cowshed, where they were detained and searched.

The following is the evidence of Lt A.R. Koe:

Having been called on to surrender, their only answer was a volley and the singing of the first three lines of 'The Soldiers' Song'. The officer in charge, Lt Hook then sent three men back for reinforcements. Firing continued intermittently until about twenty minutes past five when the Auxiliary Police reinforcements began to arrive. A few minutes after the police arrived I saw a

---

29   Diarmuid O'Leary, *WS No. 1589*, p. 7, also, Paddy Higgins, *WS No. 1467*, p. 6.
30   Paddy Higgins, *WS No. 1467*, p. 6.

constable hit by a bullet in the shoulder. Shortly after an officer climbed over the back fence with a tin of petrol and succeeded in setting fire to the roof of the house. This officer was Lt Hammond. About ten minutes later someone shouted that they were coming out. The order cease fire was given to the Crown Forces and almost immediately, six or seven men came out with their hands up. A party of Auxiliary Police and military under Lt Hook went forward from cover to accept their surrender.

As they did this I saw a man fire point blank from the window on the western side of the door, at the military party. This party immediately rushed the house past the civilians who had kept their hands up. These men then lowered their hands, scattered and attempted to escape. There were three men running down the field to the south. I shouted at them to stop. When they did not do so I ordered fire to be opened and I saw the three men fall.[31]

Taking the evidence given later during the course of the Military Court, the conclusion that I have come to is that after the men in the farmhouse agreed to surrender, Capt Higgins ordered his men to throw their loaded rifles, revolvers and spare ammunition into the open fire in the kitchen. Twelve of the fifteen in the house next marched out with their hands up as required by the Crown Forces. The combined military and police were waiting for them in the farmyard and the men had to move through them. This is when John Harty was struck down. The remaining eleven were ordered up against the east wall of the cowshed. At this stage the only shots that could have come from the house was that of the ammunition exploding in the open fire.

Suddenly and without warning, the Auxiliary Police opened fire on their prisoners and in a matter of a few seconds and before the Army officer could stop them at least six of the prisoners were shot dead. The seventh man, Jeremiah Ahern, made a dash for safety when the shooting began and managed to get about 80 metres into a field before he was shot down. Maurice Moore was later taken into the field by Lt Hook, where he identified Jeremiah Ahern.[32] Of the remainder, Patrick Higgins was shot in the mouth and William Garde and Edmond Terry were slightly wounded. Robert Walsh was the only one of the twelve not wounded. This was the only occasion when the Auxiliary Police captured an entire flying column since the destruction of the Auxiliary mobile patrol at Kilmichael twelve weeks earlier. Therefore,

31   UKNA WO 71/380, Lt A.R. Koe's evidence, pp. 36–40.
32   See, Maurice Moore's court evidence, WO 71/380.

was the killing of the prisoners at Clonmult in revenge for Kilmichael and the killings in Midleton?

The Battle of Clonmult was now over. Twelve IRA men – James Ahern, Jeremiah Ahern and his first cousin Liam Ahern, Donal Dennehy, brothers David and Michael Desmond, James Glavin, Michael Hallahan, Richard Hegarty, John Joseph Joyce, Joseph Morrissey, Christopher O'Sullivan – were dead. There were eight captured, of whom five – Paddy Higgins, Jeremiah O'Leary, John Harty, Edmond Terry and William Garde – were wounded. Jeremiah O'Leary was the only one of the five wounded during the course of the battle, the other four were wounded after surrendering. Patrick O'Sullivan, Maurice Moore and Robert Walsh were also captured and only one, Capt Jack O'Connell had escaped. The British casualty list was two military and three policemen wounded, of which one soldier and one policeman were severely wounded.

The British often refer to Clonmult as being Kilmichael in reverse, because at Kilmichael the Auxiliary mobile patrol had been wiped out and the IRA under Gen Tom Barry claimed that the Auxiliaries made a false surrender during the engagement. The British have claimed that at Clonmult the IRA made a false surrender and this is their reason for the killing of the IRA men, following their surrender.[33] Their claim is that after the first group came out of the house to surrender those remaining inside began firing on the Crown Forces.[34]

The wounded CSM, Edward Corney, was taken to Carey's house on the main road, the house searched earlier in the afternoon. While he was there waiting for transport, two of the Carey brothers, Moss and Mike, together with Mikey Sullivan, stole his blood-stained tunic and ran off with it. After removing his aide memoire from the pocket they stuffed the tunic down a rabbit burrow. The troops conducted an extensive search for the aide memoire as it contained sensitive military information, but they failed in their quest.[35]

When Capt O'Connell made his successful escape from the farmhouse, he ran down a narrow road that was running in an easterly direction for approximately 200 metres. As stated earlier, he was astonished to find that none of his comrades were with him. He returned to within sight of the farmhouse and

33 British in Ireland, Reel No. 74, Jan–March 1921, *RIC County Inspector's Monthly Confidential Report, February 1921*, CO 904/114.
34 *Ibid.*
35 Tony Moore, *Clonmult and the Creation of Legend*, p. 18.

considered attempting to get back inside.[36] He concluded that two soldiers had been detailed to pursue him, and this forced him to abandon both his intention to get back inside the farmhouse and his present location. He decided to make an attempt at locating some of the local volunteers and with them his intention was to attack the British troops from their rear and thus relieve the besieged column. He eventually met two local Volunteers, Willie Foley and another unnamed volunteer.[37] One, he sent for arms, the other he wanted to take back to the farmhouse. The individual showed extreme reluctance and eventually decided to accompany the other volunteer to fetch weapons.[38] The weapons belonging to the Clonmult Volunteers were in a farmhouse near the old cemetery in the townland of Ballyeightragh, which was only just across the valley, approximately one mile east of the battle site.[39] Neither of these two individuals returned to Clonmult prior to Jack O'Connell's departure later that evening.

John Lawton, Captain of the Clonmult Company, next arrived on the scene on a bicycle. Jack O'Connell did not realise at the time that this man was the captain of the local company.[40] Lawton informed O'Connell that the Active Service Unit (A.S.U.) of the North East Cork Battalion was located near the village of Ballynoe, six miles to the north, and he suggested going off and getting help from them.[41] Lawton eventually found the A.S.U. in the townland of Kilcronat near Ballynoe. This A.S.U. did not get to Clonmult until much later that evening, but by then they found the house on fire and the battle over.[42] They came as far as Gurteen Crossroads, just over a mile north-east of the battle site.[43] O'Connell waited for the two volunteers to return with the weapons, but in vain. He was also kept busy dodging the attention of the British soldiers that were searching for him. He finally saw the thatched roof on fire and he eventually left the area at about 6.30 pm when silence descended and he knew in his heart that the battle was over. He decided to cycle to Knockraha, which was about fourteen miles away to the west.[44]

36   Jack O'Connell, *WS No. 1444*, p. 10.
37   Jim Hegarty, interview with author.
38   Jack O'Connell, *WS No. 1444*, p. 11.
39   Jim Hegarty, interview with author.
40   Jack O'Connell, *WS No. 1444*, p. 11.
41   *Ibid.*
42   William Buckley, *WS No. 1009*, p. 17.
43   Jim Hegarty, interview with author.
44   Jack O'Connell, *WS No. 1444*, p. 15.

At about this time, the British forces would also have been making preparation to depart Clonmult. Now that the battle was over, their concern was to depart before any IRA forces would arrive. Weapons, ammunition and military equipment was recovered from the burning house and all similar items were collected from the prisoners and the dead. The eight prisoners were kept together and the entire group of both British and Irish trekked across the fields and back to the crossroads where the vehicles were parked. The bodies of the twelve IRA men were left where they had fallen. It is of interest that all travel between the crossroads and the farmhouse during the afternoon was across the fields. Even when the battle was over the British did not bring their vehicles down the road to the battle scene. This was standard procedure, as by doing so they would have been travelling into unknown territory and risking an ambush. When all of the troops, Auxiliaries, RIC and IRA men were loaded onto the vehicles, the convoy made its way to Midleton by the reverse route that they had used earlier that day.

When the reconnaissance party left Clonmult earlier that day, they travelled directly to Killacloyne, which is situated approximately two miles on the west side of Carrigtwohill, on the old main road to Cork. Just before they reached Killacloyne bridge, they turned north on to the Knockraha road and parked the car just off the junction. They proceeded to walk from the car to Cobh Junction railway station along the railway track. Having completed their reconnaissance they returned to the car with the intention of driving to the agreed rendezvous with their column at Dooneen. Dooneen is a townland about four miles north of Carrigtwohill near the village of Leamlara. While the three men were at Cobh Junction, six or seven British Army trucks passed them heading for Cork City. The men were convinced, in hindsight, that this was the same convoy that was transporting the remnants of their column as captives to Victoria Barracks in Cork City.

On approaching the car, they realised that Capt Michael Burke, of the Cobh Company, was waiting for them.[45] This in itself was not unusual, as it had been agreed that the column would be reinforced by volunteers from the Cobh Company for the proposed attack on the British at Cobh Junction. However, Burke had met an unnamed volunteer while on his way to Killacloyne, and had been informed that there had been a battle at Clonmult.[46] Burke's wife was a sister of Capt Ahern, who had been killed that afternoon at Clonmult. Comdt O'Hurley concluded that if anyone had man-

---

45   Michael Burke, *WS No. 1424*, p. 31.
46   *Ibid.*

aged to escape from Clonmult, they would make their way to Knockraha. Capt Whelan guessed that any survivor would make his way to Canavan's house in Knockraha.[47] They decided to drive there and on entering the village they met Capt O'Connell, who was with Capt Martin Corry, who was OC of the local 'E' Company.[48]

O'Connell gave them as much information as he had but at this stage he himself was not aware as to the extent of the defeat at Clonmult. The four men decided to drive back to Clonmult 'in case some of the Volunteers were still holding out'.[49] As O'Hurley remarked, 'If we cannot save them we can die with them.'[50] They, like the British, parked their car on the roadway some distance from the farmhouse and travelled across the fields. When they arrived at the site the only sound was the crackling of the still burning house.[51]

After the British had left the scene, some of the locals, including three young women, ventured to the battle site. These were two Miss Mulcahys and a Miss Allen.[52] They were accompanied by the local Catholic curate, Fr Curtin, who rendered the spiritual assistance of the Catholic Church on the bodies of the dead men.[53] Second Lt Ahern and Volunteer Stanton, both of the Dungourney Company, were at the scene when they arrived.[54] The twelve bodies had been collected and placed beside each other with their faces covered with canvas. This was how they were found by their comrades at about midnight when they returned.

Capt Whelan best described the harrowing scene:

> I undertook the heartbreaking task of uncovering their faces and identifying them, calling out each consecutively. This sad task took me some time, but between sobs of anguish, I managed it. There were two distinct pauses as I went along the row, as I had great difficulty in naming Liam Ahern (Jos. Ahern's brother) and Jerry Ahern (first cousin of Jos.) I will not even attempt to describe the mental anguish of Diarmuid O'Hurley. All four of us – Diarmuid, Jos., Jacko and myself – sobbed with a terrible grief and

47   Patrick Whelan, *WS No. 1449*, p. 53.
48   M.J. Corry, 1889–1979, Fianna Fail T.D. for East Cork, 1927–69.
49   Joseph Ahern, *WS No. 1367*, p. 52.
50   *Ibid.*
51   Patrick Whelan, *WS No. 1449*, p. 54.
52   Killeagh–Inch Historical Group, *Killeagh Parish Throughout the Ages*, p. 165.
53   Jim Hegarty, Interview with author in 2003 and 2004.
54   Joseph Ahern, *WS No. 1367*, p. 53.

sense of loss at the fate that had befallen our beloved comrades, some four or five of whom had bullet holes in the face, just below their eyes, where they had been shot by the Tans whilst prisoners. There was nothing we could do but cover their faces again, and take our sad departure to Leamlara.[55]

The four survivors spent that night in Fr Francis Flannery's house in Midleton. The distraught O'Connell was consoled by Whelan: 'That night, Jacko (Jack O'Connell) and I shared a bed. I remember putting my arm around him, to give some comfort and consolation. I believe and told him so, that he had done all that was humanly possible to save the Column.'[56]

When all of the troops, police and prisoners were loaded on to the vehicles at the crossroads, the convoy set out for Midleton. I have concluded, that at least one vehicle left earlier for Midleton to prepare for the arrival of the prisoners. This is because members of the Royal Irish Constabulary interrupted that evening's show at the cinema, cleared the building and ordered the patrons to go home, before the prisoners arrived at the RIC barracks. The cinema, which was located at the northern end of the town, adjacent to where the War of Independence monument now stands, was near the RIC barracks. At this stage, word of the battle was beginning to filter into the town and the authorities did not want a crowd in the vicinity of the Constabulary Barracks when the prisoners arrived there.

The principal reason for taking the prisoners to Midleton was to have them identified. In the event, however, only Capt Higgins was identified. Jeremiah O'Leary falsely gave his name as Murphy, and this later caused some confusion for his family. Shortly afterwards, the prisoners were put back on the trucks and transferred to Victoria Barracks. As the prisoners were being put on the trucks in Midleton, they overheard the soldiers being ordered to shoot them should any attempt be made to rescue them.

Volunteers Dan Cashman and Jack Ahern were on weekend leave from the column and both spent the Sunday in Ballinacurra, 2 kilometres south of Midleton, drilling and training the local Company. That night, when they came into Midleton, they saw lorries with military and police drawn up outside the RIC barracks.

Cashman stated:[57]

55   Patrick Whelan, *WS No. 1449*, p. 54.
56   *Ibid.*
57   Daniel Cashman, *WS No. 1523*, p. 10.

Jack suggested that we would go out on the Cork road and ambush them. We collected another Volunteer named Joe Kinsella, went out the road about a mile and a half and hurriedly built a barricade of stones on the road. We than got inside the hedge and waited for the convoy to arrive. When the military came along we blazed into them with revolvers. They burst through the barricade firing as they went and continued on to Cork. We had no idea then (about 9 pm) that the lorries contained some of our boys captured in Clonmult a few hours previously, nor had we any idea that the Column had been practically wiped out. That night we stayed at a farmer's house at Ballinacurra and it was there we learned what had happened at Clonmult, from the woman of the house.

The remainder of the journey to Cork City was uneventful and the convoy arrived in Victoria Barracks at approximately 9 pm.[58] The unwounded prisoners were lodged in the 'cage', which was a temporary holding area surrounded by barbed wire on the barrack square. The five wounded prisoners – Paddy Higgins, Jeremiah O'Leary, John Harty, Edmond Terry and William Garde – were taken to the garrison hospital. O'Leary recalls waking up from his unconscious state while having his head shaved in preparation for his head wound being attended. Paddy Higgins had his mouth wound attended, but the head of the bullet that had lodged in his upper jaw remained there. It fell out a few days later while he was sitting beside the fire in the prison. 'It was a lead bullet, not a nickel one. Had it been a nickel bullet I would not have survived.'[59]

At Clonmult the British captured a substantial quantity of weapons, ammunition and grenades belonging to the column. The total armament of the Column consisted of seventeen rifles, three shotguns, fifteen revolvers, six grenades and about 1,000 rounds of ammunition.[60] The weapons and ammunition of the reconnaissance group, the rifle taken by Jack O'Connell and the ammunition expended during the battle can be deducted from the columns arms and represents the list of equipment captured. This is mentioned in the British military communiqué, issued on Sunday evening from Dublin. However, in their second communiqué, issued on the Monday and published on Tuesday morning, it stated that the military also captured a car. Jim Hegarty, a surviving

---

58   Lt A.R. Koe's after action report, Appendix 12, (20).
59   Patrick Higgins, *WS No. 1467*, p. 6.
60   Jack O'Connell, *WS No. 1444*, p. 8.

witness to the battle, in an interview with me, also stated that he remembers the British burning a car in the farmyard that evening.[61]

There were thirteen rifles and carbines, two shotguns, twelve revolvers, 198 rounds of service ammunition, a Mills bomb, six bayonets and other equipment recovered by the British Army following the battle.[62]

61 *Military Communiqué* (British Army Headquarters, Dublin), 22nd February 1921, see Appendix 10.
62 *Cork Examiner*, Wednesday, 15th March 1921, also, Lt Dove's evidence, WO 71/380.

THE AFTERMATH OF THE BATTLE

On Monday morning, the national newspapers gave brief details of the battle and had thirteen as the number of IRA men killed.[1] However, due to the confusion of the battle, it is understandable that this incorrect figure was given. In reality, twelve IRA men had been killed and their bodies had been left overnight beside the smouldering ruin of what had been their billet at Clonmult. The British troops returned to collect the bodies on Monday morning at around 9 o'clock and carried out a more thorough search of the immediate area. The British were convinced that the body of the column commander had been removed by the IRA during the night, this gave rise to the figure of thirteen killed. The bodies were conveyed to Victoria Barracks on Monday. For the remainder of the week following the battle, the British were active around Clonmult searching for and interrogating suspects.[2]

Information on the battle gradually reached the families of the column members on Sunday night and Monday morning. The mother of the two Desmond brothers, Michael and David, was very ill in bed at her home in 17 Commissioners Buildings, Midleton. This red-brick terrace of houses on the Dungourney and Clonmult road out of Midleton, was later renamed Clonmult Terrace in honour of the three men from the terrace killed at Clonmult, the two Desmond brothers and Michael Hallahan. At about 6 pm on the Sunday evening her daughters, who were in an adjacent room, heard her speaking to someone. They went to her bedroom to find that she was alone, and they asked her to whom she was speaking. She told them that she had been speaking with

1   *Cork Examiner*, Monday, 21st February 1921.
2   British in Ireland, Reel No. 74, Jan–March 1921, *RIC County Inspector's Monthly Confidential Report, February 1921*. CO 904/114.

David and Michael, but everything was alright; they were with God. The family of Christopher O'Sullivan saw his bicycle in the back of an Army truck when it was passing through Midleton. Dick Hegarty's younger sister heard that her brother was dead when she was called out from her school classroom on the Monday morning. The distress endured by all of these families was echoed in the community.

Early the following morning, some local civilians went to the battle site to attempt to clean up the bodies. Also there was the local Catholic Curate and an 11-year-old altar boy, Michael Hennessy, whose father, John, had been one of the two men detained the previous evening at Rathorgan Crossroads. The young boy noticed some strange grey matter on the wall of the cowshed. It was only years later while killing a pig with his father that he realised that it was brain matter.[3]

The British Army arrived at the site around 9 am on Monday morning and removed the twelve unidentified bodies. The trucks were driven down a narrow lane that ran from Carey's house. The remains of the twelve dead Republicans were loaded onto the trucks and were conveyed directly to the mortuary located at the rear of the hospital block in Victoria Barracks in Cork. There they were received and labelled for identification by the military doctor on duty, Capt J.B. Morrison, Royal Army Medical Corps, (RAMC). Capt Morrison carried out an examination on all of the bodies that day.

During Monday, a special meeting of Midleton U.D.C. was held and a vote of sympathy was passed to the families of the deceased.[4] At about 11 am on Tuesday, businesses in the town began to close and to put up their shutters. That afternoon, a party of military patrolled the town and insisted that the shops must reopen. This was done, but no business was transacted.[5] Likewise, the members of Cobh U.D.C. passed a vote of sympathy and expressed their condolence to the families of the two Cobh men, Vol James Glavin and Capt James Ahern, who had been elected on to the town council for Sinn Féin the previous year. James Glavin's father wrote to the council: 'It is a source of consolation to us to realise that our son gave his life, in company with his

---

3   From his son, Sean Hennessy of Clonmult also Tony Moore, *Clonmult and the Construction of Legend*, pp. 16–17.
4   Jeremiah Falvey, *The Chronicles of Midleton 1700–1990*, p. 146.
5   *Ibid.*

gallant and brave companions, many of whom were natives of Cobh, for our dear country.'[6]

On Wednesday morning, 23rd February, a 'Military Court of Inquiry in lieu of an Inquest' was set up.[7] Its purpose was to investigate and report upon the circumstances under which the twelve civilians met their deaths. The court having assembled pursuant to order, proceeded to view the bodies of the above civilians at the Military Hospital, Cork, and to take evidence on oath. The members of the court were Capt T. Ward, 2nd Battalion, South Staffordshire Regiment and president of the inquiry, also Lt J. Hay, RASC and Lt H.W. Hall, 2nd Battalion, Hampshire Regiment.[8]

For the Crown Forces, evidence was taken on oath from Lt G.R.A. Dove and Cpl G. Carter, both of the 2nd Battalion, Hampshire Regiment. Both had been at Clonmult and they gave a general account of the events of 20th February that have already been dealt with here. Lt Dove concluded by stating that, 'There is no doubt in my mind that each one of these dead civilians was armed and took an active part in the fight.'[9]

When received into the mortuary, the twelve unidentified bodies were labelled one to twelve. The evidence and identification was carried out in that sequence.

The first to be identified was Joseph Morrissey. Ms Kitty Morrissey identified the body, and she stated on oath that she did not know where he lived or where he worked and that he was aged about 26. She did not state her relationship with the deceased.[10]

The second body to be identified was William Ahern. He was identified by his sister Agnes Ahern. She stated that he resided in The Park, Midleton, was unmarried, aged about 26, and was an accountant.

The third body to be identified was David Desmond. He was identified by his aunt, Mrs Buckley, of 16 West View, Queenstown, (Cobh). She stated that he resided in Midleton, was unmarried, aged about 24. She did not know his occupation.

The next body to be identified was Richard Hegarty. He was identified by his sister, Miss Mary Hegarty of Ladysbridge, Co. Cork. She stated that he

6   Kieran McCarthy and Maj-Britt Christensen, *Cobh's Contribution to the Fight for Irish Freedom 1913–1990*, p. 82.
7   UKNA, Kew, Military Court of Inquiry in lieu of an Inquest, WO 35/155A/53.
8   UKNA, Kew, WO 35/155A/53.
9   UKNA, Kew, Military Court of Inquiry in lieu of an Inquest, WO 35/155A/53.
10   UKNA, Kew, WO 35/155A/53.

resided in Ladysbridge, was unmarried and aged 22. He was a farmer and he was her brother.

The next body to be identified was James Ahern. He was identified by his sister, Miss Marjorie Ahern of Midleton. She stated that he was her brother, that he resided in Midleton, was unmarried, aged 24 and was an engine fitter.

The next body to be identified was John Joseph Joyce. He was identified by his sister, Miss Mary Joyce of Dunbar Street, Cork. She stated that he was her brother, resided in Midleton, was unmarried, aged 22 and was a student at the University of Cork.[11]

The seventh body to be identified was Daniel Dennehy. He was identified by Miss Christina Ahern of Midleton. She stated that he resided in Bilberry, Midleton, was unmarried, aged about 22 and was a labourer. She did not state her relationship with the deceased.

The eighth body to be identified was Jeremiah Ahern. He was identified by his sister Miss Eileen Ahern of 22 Washington Street, Cork City. She stated that he was her brother, that he resided in Midleton, was unmarried, aged 22 and was a mechanic.

The next body to be identified was Michael Hallahan. He was identified by Miss Nellie Mackey of Queenstown, (Cobh). She stated that he resided in Midleton, was unmarried, aged about 22 and was a tailor. She did not state her relationship with the deceased.

The tenth body to be identified was Christopher O'Sullivan. He was identified by Miss Francis O'Sullivan of Midleton. She stated that he was her brother, that he resided in Midleton, was unmarried, aged about 27 and had no occupation.

The eleventh body to be identified was James Glavin. He was identified by his mother, Mrs Kate Glavin of Midleton. She stated that he was her son and that he resided in Midleton, was unmarried, aged about 19 and that he was a clerk.

The last body to be identified was Michael Desmond. He was identified by his aunt, Mrs Buckley of 16 West View, Queenstown, Cobh. She stated that he resided in Midleton, was unmarried, aged 22 and was employed at Hanlons of Cork. She did not know his occupation.[12]

---

11   UKNA, Kew, WO 35/155A/53.
12   UKNA, Military Court of Inquiry in lieu of an Inquest, WO 35/155A/53.

Having considered the evidence and on concluding as to the cause of death in each case, the finding of the court, naming the twelve deceased and their details, was:

That the shots causing the deaths of the twelve named civilians were fired by the Crown Forces in the execution of their duty.

That at the time of meeting their deaths, the twelve named civilians were taking part in active operations against Forces of the Crown in the nature of armed resistance.

That no blame whatever attached in the matter to the Forces of the Crown or to any member thereof.

Signed at Cork this 24th day of February 1921.
T Ward, Capt
2nd Battalion South Staffordshire Regt
President of the Military Court of Inquiry in lieu of an Inquest.[13]

On Wednesday, 23rd February, the bodies were released to their families and were removed from Victoria Barracks late that evening. The cortege carrying the twelve coffins travelled together as far as Cobh Cross and from there the coffins of James Ahern and James Glavin were taken to St Colman's Cathedral in Cobh. The other ten coffins were taken to Midleton by lorry, where they arrived at about 10 pm.

Crowds had been gathering in the town from 4 pm and the church bell had been ringing since about that time. It was a fine, dry, calm night, though somewhat cold, and a deep silence pervading the whole scene at such an hour at night, the event was undoubtedly solemn, and was one calculated never to be forgotten by those who were present on the sad occasion.[14]

The coffins were shouldered from the Cork side of the town to the church, where they were placed in front of the high altar. Following Requiem High Mass at 10 am on Thursday, 24th February, the nine coffins of the local men were laid to rest in the Republican plot. The coffins were draped in tricolours

---

13   UKNA, WO 35/155A/53.
14   Jeremiah Falvey, *The Chronicles of Midleton*, p. 146.

and there were innumerable wreaths.[15] The tenth coffin, Dick Hegarty's, was conveyed to Ballymacoda, near Youghal. On the same day, at 3 p.m. the funerals of the two Cobh men were held in Cobh Cathedral and they were buried in the Republican plot of what is now the old graveyard at Ticknock, on the northern side of the town. On Friday, Dick Hegarty was laid to rest beside the church in Ballymacoda.

Diarmuid O'Hurley, Joseph Ahern, Paddy Whelan and Jack O'Connell spent the Monday night in Midleton, in Fr Francis Flannery's house and on the Thursday, attended the funerals.[16] Ahern said, 'When the internment had been completed, O'Hurley drew his gun, signalled to Paddy Whelan and O'Connell to do likewise, and we then gave our last salute by firing three volleys over the grave. We then made our way quickly out of the graveyard.'[17]

As previously mentioned, when Jeremiah O'Leary was taken into the RIC barracks in Midleton for possible identification, he gave a false name, possibly Murphy. His mother and sister were convinced he was lying dead somewhere. They went as far as purchasing a burial plot for him and holding a wake. Eventually, he wrote to his mother telling her that he was a prisoner in the Detention Barracks.[18]

A closer inspection of the official RIC report of the battle illustrates the overall effectiveness of the IRA campaign in neutralising this once efficient force, despite their defeat at Clonmult. Two weeks after the battle, the RIC still had not corrected the number of IRA men killed, and more noticeable, still believed that the column commander, Diarmuid O'Hurley, had been killed at Clonmult: 'The leader of the rebel gang – Jeremiah Hurley – (English translation for Diarmuid), who had been operating in this District for a considerable time is believed to have been killed in this attack, but the body was taken away during the night. It was the only body removed.'[19]

The five wounded prisoners of the battle spent some time in the Military Hospital, in Victoria Barracks, before being lodged in the Military Detention Barracks to join their three unwounded colleagues. Seven of the eight men did

---

15   *Ibid.*
16   Later, Canon Francis Flannery, Castlemartyr.
17   Joseph Ahern, *WS No. 1367*, p. 53.
18   Diarmuid O'Leary, *WS No. 1589*, pp. 8–9.
19   British in Ireland, Reel No. 74, Jan–March 1921, *RIC County Inspector's Monthly Confidential Report, February 1921*, CO 904/114.

not have long to wait for their trial. Due to the gunshot wound to his mouth, Paddy Higgins, the eighth prisoner, remained in hospital and was judged as being medically unfit to be tried alongside his comrades. However, his turn would come later, on 21st June 1921.

THE TRIAL BY MILITARY COURT OF THE CLONMULT PRISONERS

Within the Martial Law area the military authorities had a number of options available to them for trying civilian prisoners for charges against the Restoration of Order in Ireland Act, 1920. At the lower end of the scale was the Summary Court, (SC). This court could impose up to six months' imprisonment, with or without hard labour, impose a fine up to £100, recommend an accused for internment or refer the case for trial by Military Court.[1]

A Field General Court Martial (FGCM) of civilians in the Martial Law area was cumbersome and slow. The Military Court was swifter and less cumbersome. The military High Command also believed, incorrectly as it later transpired, that the Military Court was not subject to interference by the High Court. Where charges were punishable by death, the FGCM was required to include a person with legal knowledge and experience; the Military Court was not. The FGCM could only pass a sentence available under common law. The Military Court could impose their own sentence. Where a FGCM imposed the death penalty, clemency was the preserve of the Lord Lieutenant. With the Military Court, the Army reserved the question of clemency to the Commander in Chief.[2] The Clonmult prisoners were tried by Military Court.

Another option was the drumhead court martial, used on a maximum of three occasions during 1921. All of the individuals officiating at such a hearing were British Army officers. The IRA prisoner was defended by a British officer, the jurors were British Army officers and the judge–advocate was a senior army officer. The first occasion that a captured IRA prisoner was tried by drumhead court martial in the martial law area was on Monday,

---

1   Sean Enright, *The Trial of Civilians by Military Courts 1921*, p. 34.
2   *Ibid*. pp. 37–38.

2nd May 1921. The day before, a Crown Forces mobile patrol was ambushed near Kildorrery in north Cork at approximately 5.30 pm. The patrol over-whelmed the ambush party and in the ensuing battle two IRA men were killed. Volunteer Patrick Casey was spotted by two soldiers firing his rifle. After firing a round at the same two soldiers, the IRA man dropped his rifle and surrendered. He was taken to Victoria Barracks, where he was tried by drumhead court martial the following day, he was found guilty and sentenced to death. He was executed at 6 pm that evening. The entire process from cap-ture to execution took twenty-five hours.

From August 1920, internment was also available to the authorities throughout the island of Ireland and not confined to the Martial Law area.[3] By the early part of 1921, the vast majority of Republicans held in cus-tody were internees. Those Republicans that on conviction received short custodial sentences could on or before their release date be reclassified as internees and thus kept in custody. Internees continued to be held in the internment camps until after the Anglo-Irish Treaty was signed in December 1921. The convicted Republican prisoners were released after the Treaty was ratified in January 1922.

On 1st March, a summary of the evidence against seven of the men cap-tured at Clonmult was taken in Victoria Barracks, Cork. The eighth, Paddy Higgins, was still medically unfit to stand trial. The trial of the accused by Military Court began in the gymnasium of Victoria Barracks, on Tuesday, 8th March.[4] The Military Court officials consisted of three British Army officers adjudicating. There was no requirement for any of these officers to be legally trained, but the most senior had to hold the substantive rank of captain.[5] A British Army judge-advocate, Capt F.E. Young, was present to provide legal advice to the prosecutors, and the prosecutor for the Crown was Maj W.C. Gover, O.B.E., HQ 6th Division legal branch. A death sen-tence required the unanimous verdict of all three judges. It could not be carried out, however, until it was confirmed by the Commander-in-Chief, the Forces in Ireland, Gen Macready.[6] The President of the Military Court

3   William Murphy, *Political Imprisonment and the Irish, 1912–1921*, p. 193.
4   *Irish Times*, 9th March 1921.
5   Brian Barton, *From Behind a Closed Door, Secret Court Martial Records of the 1916 Easter Rising*, p. 20.
6   *Ibid*. p. 28.

Members of the flying column of the 4th Battalion, 1st Cork Brigade, 1921.
Left to right: Michael Desmond★, Paddy Higgins, James Glavin★, Donal Dennehy★, Joseph Ahern,
Richard Hegarty★, Joseph Morrissey★, Michael Hallahan★, David Stanton and Patrick White.
★ Killed during the Battle of Clonmult.

Left to right: Comdt Joseph Ahern, Midleton, Vol Richard Hegarty, Garryvoe, killed at Clonmult and Capt Paddy Higgins, wounded at Clonmult after surrendering.

It was members of the Auxiliary Division RIC (ADRIC) that reinforced the British Army and carried out the killing of the prisoners at Clonmult.

Capt Jack O'Connell, acting column commander at Clonmult and the only member to escape.

Capt Paddy Whelan, a member of the reconnaissance group.

Vol Christopher O'Sullivan, killed at Clonmult.

Left to right: John Harty, Cloyne, Diarmuid 'Sonny' O'Leary, Killeagh, Patrick Higgins, Rostellan, and Edmund Terry, Churchtown South, all four captured at Clonmult. Photo taken at Clonmult graveyard, February 1971, on the fiftieth anniversary of the battle.

Four views of the ruin of the farmhouse at Clonmult following the battle.

The February 1935 Battle of Clonmult commemoration, marching through Main Street in Midleton. From *Irish Examiner* archives.

Re-internment of the remains of Comdt Diarmuid O'Hurley from Churchtown North cemetery to the Republican Plot in Midleton, September 1921.

Comdt D. O'Hurley, column commander, killed by Crown Forces, north of Midleton, 28th May 1921.

Second from the left, Black and Tan Constable Harold Thompson attached to Midleton RIC was shot dead in Midleton as a reprisal for the execution of the two Clonmult prisoners. Photo from *Rebel Cork's Fighting Story*.

Cronin's public house, Clonmult, burned down by Crown Forces as an official reprisal for the killing of the two Black and Tans in Castlemartyr wood.

Diarmuid 'Sonny' O'Leary, captured at Clonmult, convicted and sentenced to death. His sentence was later commuted to penal servitude for life.

The fourteen members of the column who lost their lives as a result of the Battle of Clonmult. Front, left to right: Donal Dennehy, Liam Ahern, David Desmond and Maurice Moore★. Middle: James Glavin, John Joe Joyce, James Ahern and Michael Desmond. Back: Richard Hegarty, Jeremiah Ahern, Christopher O'Sullivan, Joseph Morrissey, Michael Hallahan and Patrick O'Sullivan★. ★ Captured at Clonmult and later executed.

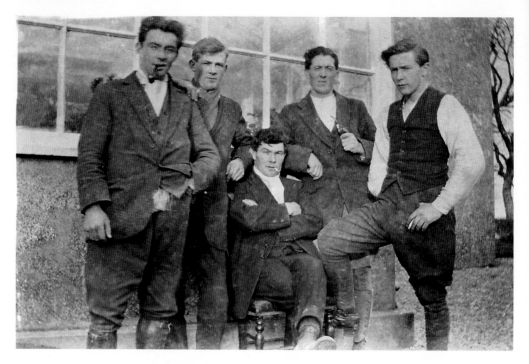

Left to right: Vol Dan Cashman, Midleton, he was in Walsh's house in Cloyne when the column was surrounded; Vol Michael Desmond, killed at Clonmult; Vol Jack Ahern, died in 1923, his brother Michael was killed by Crown Forces as a reprisal for an ambush in Midleton; Vol Tom Buckley; and Vol James Glavin, killed at Clonmult.

Vol James Glavin, Cobh, killed at Clonmult. The photos were taken at Conway's, Garryvoe, where the column stayed after the escape from Cloyne.

Vice-Comdt Joe Ahern, second-in-command of the column and a member of the reconnaissance group.

Vol John Joe Joyce, Midleton, killed in the opening action with Crown Forces at Clonmult.

Richard Barry and John Ryan were both killed by soldiers from the Cameron Highlanders Regiment as reprisals for the killings of members of the Crown Forces following the executions of the two Clonmult prisoners.

Lt A.R. Koe and Lt G.R.A. Dove, two of the officers of the Hampshire Regiment present at Clonmult for the entire battle.

Vol Michael Desmond, killed in the opening action against Crown Forces at Clonmult.

CSM E. Corney, M.M., 2nd Battalion, Hampshire Regiment, wounded in the shoulder by Capt Jack O'Connell during his escape from the house.

Maj Compton-Smith was executed by the IRA as a reprisal for the British execution of the Clonmult and Mourne Abbey prisoners.

Ex-Gnr Michael O'Keeffe, a retired soldier and First World War veteran, was killed by the IRA in Carrigtwohill in reprisal for the execution of the Clonmult prisoners.

Volunteer William Bransfield. Killed by Crown Forces in Carrigtwohill as a reprisal for the IRA killing of members of the Crown Forces following the Clonmult executions. Vol Bransfield and ex-Gnr Michael O'Keeffe were married to two sisters.

A painting of Richard (Dick) Hegarty, killed at Clonmult, from the Hegarty family archives.

Robert Walsh from Ballycotton, captured at Clonmult.

Edmond Terry from Churchtown South, captured at Clonmult.

William Garde from Ballynamona near Ballycotton, as a 17-year-old was captured at Clonmult.

Front, left to right: Michael Cotter, lady ?, Michael Hennessy, Michael Burke, Tommy Wallis, Jack Hegarty, brother of Dick, Edmond Terry, captured at Clonmult and last two unidentified.
Rear: first two unidentified, ? Ahern, unidentified, Michael Murphy, Michael Kearney, Peter Hegarty, brother of Dick, Michael Murnane, three unidentified, 'Kruger' White, John Harty, captured at Clonmult.

was Lt Col C.B.Vandeleur, DSO.[7] Lt Col Vandeleur sat as president in trials that resulted in eleven executions.[8]

The seven accused, William Garde, aged 18 of Ballinamona; John Harty, aged 19 of Ballyroe, Cloyne; Edmond Terry, aged 17 of Churchtown South; Maurice Moore, aged 25 of Queenstown; Robert Walsh, aged 20 of Ballycotton; Patrick O'Sullivan, aged 24 of Queenstown; and Jeremiah O'Leary, aged 19 of Killeagh, all civilians in the county of Cork, were charged ...

> with committing an offence in that they, at Clonmult, in the County Cork, on the 20th day of February, 1921, did, with other persons unknown, levy war against His Majesty by attacking with arms a detachment of His Majesty's Forces.
>
> To be tried by Military Court,
>
> > Signed, E P Strickland, Major General
> > Commanding 6th Division & Military Governor[9]
> > 7/3/21

Mr Michael Comyn, K.C., instructed by Mr C.K. Murphy, solicitor, Cork, appeared for William Garde, Robert Walsh, Edmond Terry and John Harty. Mr Joseph McCarthy, B.L., instructed by Mr Maurice O'Connor, solicitor, Cork, represented Maurice Moore, Patrick O'Sullivan and Jeremiah (Diarmuid) O'Leary. During the court and in court records Diarmuid O'Leary was referred to as Jeremiah, the English translation of his name.

The accused men all pleaded not guilty. In opening the case, the prosecutor produced a proclamation, issued by the Military Governor, prescribing the County of Cork as a Martial Law area, and pointing out that persons convicted of certain offences were liable to suffer the penalty of death.[10]

On 10th December 1920 the Lord Lieutenant had proclaimed the following areas to be under and subject to Martial Law: the County of Cork (East Riding), the County of Cork (West Riding), the County of the City of Cork, the County of Tipperary (North Riding), the County of Tipperary (South Riding), the County of Kerry, the County of Limerick and the County of the City of Limerick.[11]

---

7   UKNA, Kew, London, Clonmult case file, WO 71/380.
8   Sean Enright, *The Trial of Civilians by Military Courts, Ireland 1921*, p. 40.
9   *Cork Examiner*, 9th March 1921, also, Clonmult WO 71/380.
10   *Irish Times*, 9th March 1921 and WO 71/380.
11   Clonmult, WO 71/380.

On 4th January 1921, Gen Macready, Commanding-in-Chief the Forces in Ireland, issued Proclamation No. 2 extending Martial Law to County Clare, County Waterford, City of Waterford, County Wexford and County Kilkenny. This came into force one week later, on 11th January.[12]

The details of the events that occurred at Clonmult on the day of the battle were presented by the prosecution. After this, evidence was tendered by the military doctor, Capt W.L. Young, Royal Army Medical Corps (RAMC), who was on duty in the Military Hospital in Victoria Barracks on the evening of 20th February. He stated that:

At approximately 9.30 pm, five wounded prisoners, Edmond Terry, John Harty, Patrick Higgins, William Garde and Jeremiah O'Leary all civilians, were brought in under escort, suffering from gunshot wounds. All had received some medical aid before their arrival at the hospital, none of the wounds were serious. William Garde had a bullet wound in the forearm, a flesh wound. John Harty had a gunshot wound (GSW) in his head, Capt Young was not certain that it was a gunshot wound. It did not present the appearance of having been caused by the blow of a rifle. It was a very small skin wound. It might have been caused by a light blow or splinter. The blow could not possibly have stunned him. Edmond Terry had a flesh wound in his forearm and a small wound on his ribs on his left side. Jeremiah O'Leary had a gunshot wound in his head. There were two wounds. The bullet went through his scalp and touched bone. It was on top of his head. He would get it from a bullet if he was lying down. In my opinion it was not a ricochet. He concluded that, if at the front these men would not have got beyond a dressing station. The men were admitted to the Military Hospital for about ten days. About the same time the sergeant-major of the 2nd Hampshire Regiment CSM Corney and one unnamed RIC constable were also admitted and treated for gunshot wounds received at Clonmult.[13]

The next witness for the prosecution was Lt G.R.A. Dove, 2nd Battalion, Hampshire Regiment, who was present during the battle. He gave details of the deployment of the troops after they left the vehicles at Rathorgan Crossroads, the cordon and search of the first house and the encirclement of the second house.

---

12   Clonmult Military Court file, WO 71/380.
13   *Ibid*. Capt Young's evidence.

The patrol he was with was about 250 metres from the farmhouse when he heard the shots that resulted in the deaths of Michael Desmond and John Joe Joyce. The patrol was about 100 metres from the house when he saw the soldiers from the other patrol. Shortly afterwards he saw the bodies of the two civilians. Just as the two patrols linked up, he suddenly saw the four men that ran out the front door. The four men ran towards a barn. Two at least were armed with service rifles and two had either carbines or shotguns. He stated: 'We opened fire on these four, two fell and the other two got into the barn.' None of the military witnesses saw Capt Jack O'Connell leave the farmhouse. Desultory firing continued for about three-quarters of an hour. He confirmed that Auxiliary Police reinforcements arrived from Midleton at approximately 5.20 pm, the setting fire to the roof of the building and the subsequent surrender approximately fifteen minutes later. He further stated that after the roof was set on fire bombs were thrown through the roof. He stated that there were shots fired from the building immediately after the first group of IRA men emerged to surrender and that in the melee that followed these men were shot while attempting to escape. The remainder were taken prisoner at approximately 6 pm.

These prisoners were marched across the fields to the lorries, taken to the RIC barracks in Midleton and later to Victoria Barracks. He was able to identify to the court Edmond Terry, Maurice Moore, Robert Walsh, Patrick O'Sullivan and Jeremiah O'Leary as being among the prisoners taken.[14] During cross-examination he further stated that he was second-in-command of the military party approaching from the west. He further stated that it was Lt Hammond that crept up to the house and called on those inside to come out. He did not know if any of the three other officers guaranteed their lives if they surrendered. During the lulls he also called on the men to surrender. He neither heard any of those inside ask for surrender terms nor heard any of the officers tell those inside that they would not be shot. He was at the west side of the house with the Auxiliary Police when the six or seven civilians came out with their hands up. About two minutes later others came out of the house. They did not have their hands up. Afterwards he went into the house and saw rifles, carbines and other equipment lying around.

Cross-examined, he stated: 'that he saw eleven dead bodies, four of whom he himself saw being shot. He saw the bodies again at 9 o'clock the next morning, they were laid out on the road next to the house.'

---

14   *Cork Examiner*, 9th March 1921 and WO 71/380, Lt G.R.A. Dove's evidence.

Re-examined by the prosecutor, he stated that: 'Some of the men surrendered with their hands up, then put their hands down and attempted to escape. None of those shot in the melee had their hands up. The end came around 6.30 pm.'[15]

The third witness, Lt D.F. Hook, M.C., 2nd Battalion, Hampshire Regiment, officer in charge of the military at Clonmult, gave similar evidence. He was the overall commander of the military at Clonmult and also in command of the patrol that approached from the west with Lt Dove. He saw the three or four civilians run out of the house and saw two of them being shot down. He later saw the two dead civilians at the back of the house; one had a service rifle the other a carbine or shotgun and both had a revolver in a holster around their waists. He stated that:

> after the initial engagements there was infrequent firing on both sides. About an hour after the fight started, he sent three men to Midleton for reinforcements and they returned with approximately twenty-four Auxiliary Police. On their arrival the firing from the Crown Forces intensified and attempts were made to throw bombs through the windows. He was hit by a bullet fired from the house but it did not penetrate his uniform. He witnessed the firing of the thatch about ten minutes after the reinforcements arrived. Shortly afterwards he heard a policeman call on those inside to surrender. He saw six or eight civilians come out with their hands up. Lt Hook stated that he went forward with some of his men to take the surrender of the first group to emerge from the house. While doing so, two or three shots were fired as far as he could judge from the house. The civilians rushed forward and some were shot. When it was over he found that he had eight prisoners, some of whom were wounded. He later entered the house and saw collected there, twelve rifles and carbines, some shotguns and revolvers and a good deal of mixed ammunition.

He identified prisoners Edmond Terry, Maurice Moore and Robert Walsh.[16] He also stated that while they were searching the house the roof was still burning and that there were several explosions.[17] This would have been live ammunition detonating in the open fireplace.[18]

---

15   *Cork Examiner*, 9th March 1921 and WO 71/380, Lt G.R.A. Dove's evidence.
16   Clonmult, WO 71/380, Lt Hook's evidence, pp. 49–50.
17   UKNA, WO 71/380, Lt Hook's evidence, pp. 49–50.
18   Prior to surrendering some threw their weapons and ammunition into the fireplace.

During cross-examination much of his evidence was as from Lt Dove. In addition, on one occasion he called on the men to surrender and the reply he received was a shot from the house. He confirmed that Lt Hammond fired the thatch on the north side. He witnessed the surrender and the stampede of the prisoners, who he stated may have been frightened or trying to escape. He further stated that: 'The men rushed across the yard after the shots were fired behind them. If the six men were trying to escape, I would have been justified in firing on them.' He could not identify any of the prisoners in court as having been in the first party to surrender. Following his re-examination, at 5 pm on 8th March, the court was adjourned.

When the court reassembled the following morning, evidence was taken from British soldiers that were present at Clonmult. Pte A. Murhall, 2nd Battalion, Hampshire Regiment, was called to give his evidence. Immediately defence counsel formally objected because in accordance with Statute Law, Pte Murhall's name, profession and his place of abode had not been supplied to the defence. Mr McCarthy, also for the defence, supported this objection and further claimed that the Proclamation of Martial Law had no force and the court must rely on Statute Law of England. The court over-ruled the objections.[19]

The fourth witness, Pte Murhall, stated under oath that he had been detailed to fire on the only window at the rear of the house, from where he had seen a man sniping at the soldiers. Towards dusk he heard shots and shouting from the front of the house. He saw seven civilians lined up near a shed. He remembered seeing all of the accused then present in the court – with the exception of Maurice Moore and John Harty – as being present at Clonmult. At the request of counsel for the accused, the witness left the court and the accused's positions in the court was changed before the last question was answered by the witness.[20]

The fifth witness, Pte C. Sherry, 2nd Battalion, Hampshire Regiment, identi-fied all of the accused in court with the exception of the accused, John Harty. He was a member of Lt Koe's patrol. He was involved in the initial engagement and was firing for approximately five minutes before they were reinforced by the second patrol. He was later positioned about 10 metres from the back of the house. He was one of the three men sent to Midleton for reinforcements. When he returned he took up a position at the front of the house. He heard and obeyed the order to cease fire just before the first civilians came out. As

19   UKNA, WO 71/380, Pte Murhall's evidence.
20   *Ibid.*

they came out he stated that fire was opened on them from the window of the house. The prisoners then scattered. There were men killed after the ceasefire who tried to escape. The seven or eight that surrendered in the second party did not try to escape and were taken prisoner.[21]

The sixth witness, a Black and Tan, RIC Constable A.B.D. Smith attached to Cornmarket Street RIC Barracks in Cork City, was next called. He stated that he was present about dusk on the 20th when certain civilians were arrested at a farmhouse in Clonmult. He also stated that after the surrender he saw several rifles, revolvers and ammunition lying about in the yard. He identified all of the prisoners with the exception of John Harty and Jeremiah O'Leary as being at Clonmult. He first saw the men after they were taken prisoner. He accompanied them to Midleton and he did not travel to Victoria Barracks. Cross-examined, he stated that before the ceasefire he was positioned at the north side of the house.[22]

The seventh witness called was a second Black and Tan, RIC Constable Henry Harris, also of Cornmarket Street RIC. He was part of the reinforcements that arrived during the battle. He was present at approximately 6 pm when the surrender took place. He identified all of the prisoners with the exception of Jeremiah O'Leary as being present at Clonmult. They were searched when he saw them, and were already prisoners. They surrendered about a quarter of an hour after the house was set on fire. He noticed several bicycles in the yard.

Re-examined by the prosecutor, he stated that on that day he started out from Cork. When he left he didn't know where he was going.[23]

The eighth witness, Sergeant S.E.T. Mantle, 2nd Battalion, Hampshire Regiment, was the NCO in charge of the main guard at Victoria Barracks on the day of the battle. At about 9 pm, four civilians were brought to the guard room and he secured three of them there. The fourth was wounded and he sent him to the hospital. The prisoner told him that he was about 17 years of age.[24]

The next witness, the ninth for the prosecution, Lt Hammond, was not on the list of witnesses. Counsel for the accused requested his attendance and this was granted by the court. Lt. H. Hammond, M.C., was the Brigade Intelligence Officer of the 17th Infantry Brigade and was an officer of the

---

21   UKNA, WO 71/380, Pte Sherry's evidence.
22   UKNA, WO 71/380, RIC Constable Smith's evidence.
23   UKNA, WO 71/380, RIC Constable Harris's evidence.
24   UKNA, WO 71/380, Sgt Mantles's evidence.

Royal Field Artillery (RFA). He stated that he was with the first group to reach the house and they had approached from the south-west. He later saw two bodies at the front of the house and two at the back. After setting fire to the roof, he moved to the front corner on the east side of the house. This is where he was when the men came out. He confirmed that an order to cease fire had been given to the military before the men came out of the house. When all were out of the house, he carried out a search inside. He confirmed that there were no bodies in the house. He saw two bodies at the rear of the house and two at the front. He saw weapons about the house and in the yard. During re-examination by the prosecutor he stated that it was he who set fire to the roof and also that none of the troops present were under his command.[25] He was extra-regimentally employed. He did not see the faces of the men as they came out because he was to the side and behind them. He also stated that when the men came out, a shot was fired and the men scattered in all directions.[26]

At 5 pm on 12th March 1921 the court adjourned. At 10 am on the 14th it reassembled, present with the same members as on the 12th.[27]

The next witness, Lt Koe, was also not on the list of witnesses. Counsel for the accused requested his attendance and this too was granted by the court. He stated that he had been on leave since shortly after 20th February and had been recalled from leave. He stated that he was in charge of the military patrol that included Lt Hammond, a CSM and six men, and that they approached the house from the south-west. When they were about 30 yards from the house he saw a number of bicycles in the yard and a number of men running backwards and forwards inside the door of the house. He deployed five of his men to line a ditch on the south side of the house, to cover the front door. He decided to move east around the house along with the CSM and one soldier, and they were crossing in front of the small copse of trees on the east side of the house when fire was opened on them from the wood. (This was shortly after Jack O'Connell had emerged from the house.) He saw a civilian armed with a rifle firing at him from approximately 25 yards (20 metres). Shots were exchanged between the soldiers and a civilian (Jack O'Connell). After about three minutes of firing CSM Corney was wounded in the shoulder. Lt Koe, the wounded CSM and the soldier ran back to cover in the lane that ran east from the house. Lt Koe

---

25   *Cork Examiner*, 14th March 1921 and Clonmult WO 71/380.
26   UKNA, WO 71/380, Lt Hammond's evidence.
27   UKNA, WO 71/380.

and the other two then moved around to the north side of the house and then back to where he linked up with the remainder of his patrol that had been reinforced by the second patrol. He saw two bodies lying at the rear of the house and two in the front yard. There were rifles or shotguns on the ground beside all four.[28]

He further stated that Lt Hook, the third witness, had called on those inside to surrender. The response was a volley of fire and the singing of three lines of 'The Soldiers' Song'. At this stage three soldiers were sent by Lt Hook to Midleton for reinforcements. He further stated there was infrequent firing from the house until about twenty minutes past five, when the police reinforcements began to arrive. He saw one of these policemen being wounded by a bullet in the shoulder. He also saw Lt Hammond climb over the fence with a can of petrol to set fire to the thatch roof. Very shortly afterwards those inside decided to surrender. He then went to the front of the house and saw the first group emerge with their hands up. When they came out he saw one of those still inside the window on the left of the door fire at point-blank range at the military taking the surrender. Some of the prisoners scattered and attempted to escape. He called on them to stop and, not doing so, he next ordered the troops to fire at them and he saw three of them fall. After a few minutes he returned, where he found eight prisoners in the south-west corner of the farmyard.[29] He took two unwounded prisoners (Maurice Moore and one other) round to identify the rebels killed, which they did. All then made their way to the lorries and left the area.

In cross-examination he stated that he was not in charge of the military party at Clonmult, Lt Hook was. He did not witness the shooting of the four men that he saw lying on the ground. He was in the lane at the time and he stayed in the lane for about two minutes. He heard his men firing at about the same time as he was firing on the civilian in the wood.[30]

Lt G.R.A. Dove, previously examined, was recalled. He had made out the original list of arms, ammunition and equipment found at the farmhouse on an envelope that he subsequently lost. The list included thirteen rifles and carbines, two shotguns, twelve revolvers, 198 rounds of service ammunition, a Mills bomb, bayonets and equipment. Some items were found on the dead bodies and more was found on the table and on chairs in the house. While

---

28   UKNA, WO 71/380, Lt Koe's evidence.
29   *Cork Examiner*, 15th March 1921 and WO 71/380.
30   UKNA, WO 71/380, Lt Koe's evidence.

they were searching the house there were several explosions; the house was still on fire.[31]

The prosecution then closed.

Opening the defence, Mr Comyn made the following submission arguing points of law:[32]

That the offence charged is not triable by a Military Court, and reads Proclamation No. 2, asserts that there is nothing in the two Proclamations produced entitling the Court to try a charge of levying war.

That the charge of levying war is not proved. Points out no proof of insurrection, that the people outside never saw those inside and that the house was first fired by those outside.

That no proof has been given of the serving on the accused of a list of witnesses at any time in accordance with Statutes.

The prosecution replied as follows:

That Military Court is not limited in any way by an offence coming within a particular Proclamation and that in the Martial Law area every offence is triable by Military Court.

That ample evidence to justify Court in finding accused guilty unless they can establish their defence.

That question of giving list of witnesses has already been overruled by Court and this point might only be a cause of objection if accused were tried by Civil Court.

The court ruled as follows:

On first submission that charge is triable by Military Court.

That the Court desires the defence to proceed.

That third submission is already over-ruled and no further comment necessary.[33]

Mr Comyn addressed the court for the defence. Reading Manual of Military Law (MML), he drew attention to the fact that these men were offered some

---

31   *Cork Examiner*, 15th March 1921 and UKNA, WO 71/380, Lt Dove's evidence.

32   UK PRO, WO 71/380.

33   *Ibid.*

inducement, i.e. that they would not be shot if they surrendered, that arms found were insufficient to arm all the persons there, that there was evidence that all the firing could have been done by five or six men, and that the accused were in the house accidently and were unarmed.[34]

Opening the case for the defence, one of the accused, Edmond Terry, stated that he was 17 years of age, came from Churchtown (South) and was a carpenter's apprentice. He further stated that he was not a member Sinn Féin, Irish Volunteers, Fianna, nor of the IRA. His evidence was that he attended mass in Churchtown South at 9.30 a.m. and afterwards he met the accused, John Harty. After mass Terry went to Hennessy's to buy cigarettes for his grandmother, Mrs Ellen Fitzgerald, who lived in Clonmult. He told Harty that he was due to visit his grandmother and they decided that they would both go to Clonmult that afternoon. They both went to Harty's for their dinner. Terry had borrowed his own brother's bicycle for the journey. They set off for Clonmult about 1.15 pm, going via Cloyne, and continuing on their way they met the accused Robert Walsh and William Garde at Ladysbridge. From there, the four cycled to Clonmult, arriving there at around 2.30 pm. Terry went to his grandmother's house, which was at the crossroads in the village, and while there drank a cup of tea. Meanwhile, the other three waited outside the house, where they met Dick Hegarty. Later Hegarty brought the four of them to the farmhouse. The four boys remained in the farmyard of the farmhouse and Hegarty went inside.

'They were at the farmhouse about ten minutes when someone shouted at them to come inside, immediately after this the shooting started.' Terry further stated that he spent the duration of the battle on the floor, between the window and the door. After about two hours he heard someone shout, 'On what conditions will we surrender, will we be shot?' The answer came, 'No, come out with your hands up.' He emerged from the house after the surrender with his hands up. He saw police and soldiers in the yard and he was ordered up against the wall of the cowshed. Shortly afterwards he heard shots and he saw three or four of the prisoners fall and it was at this stage he received the three gunshot wounds, two in the stomach and one in the wrist.[35] Later, after being searched, he was marched across the fields to the trucks. He spent three days, from Sunday to Wednesday, in the military hospital in Victoria Barracks.[36]

---

34 WO 71/380.
35 *Cork Examiner*, 15th March 1921 and WO 71/380.
36 *Cork Examiner*, 15th March 1921 and WO 71/380, Edmond Terry's evidence.

Cross-examined by the prosecutor, he further stated that he was not a member of the Boys' Brigade or Fianna. He said he had known John Harty, William Garde and Robert Walsh for a number of years. He didn't know Hegarty. He later heard his Christian name, Richard, but some of the others called him Dick. He thought there were two rooms and the kitchen downstairs in the farmhouse and one room upstairs. When he came out of the house he was fifth in line. He didn't know who was first, William Garde was second and John Harty was third and he didn't know who was fourth. They were pushed by the police towards the wall of the cowshed. He didn't see anyone trying to get away. Nine or ten of them were eventually lined up against the wall with their hands up. The police were standing in front of them with soldiers to the side. The police, from yards in front of them, started firing at them. This was when he was wounded, one of the bullets going through his wrist. He stated that he then fell completely unconscious.[37]

The first witness on Tuesday, 15th March, was Mrs Mary Josephine Terry, mother of Edmond. She had five other sons, the eldest being 23. She stated that Edmond was 17 in April 1920 and that he was apprenticed to David McGuire and due out of his time in May 1921. She stated that her son was a steady boy and in no way a wild boy. She confirmed that her mother, Mrs Fitzgerald, lived in Clonmult and that two of her daughters, Ellen and Nora, lived with her. She corroborated the evidence given by her son, and added that before both of them went to 9.30 am mass she had given him money for 'fags' for his grandmother. She stated that he borrowed a friend's bicycle, as his own was out of order. She knew John Harty very well and had only heard of William Garde and Robert Walsh from her son.[38]

David McGuire was the next witness and he stated he was a general carpenter and that the accused had been indentured to him as an apprentice since 14th May 1917. The accused lived in David McGuire's house during the week because they started work at 7 am and worked late in the evening and as he was indentured he was entitled to free board. He said that Edmond Terry was a hard-working boy and would not have time for philandering about, was not a member of any illegal organisation, and he had never seen guns in his possession.

Cross-examined by the prosecutor about Edmond Terry's bicycle, he stated his had been out of order for a few months and it was in his workshop. He had borrowed his brother's. He needed a bicycle to run errands.[39]

---

37 WO 71/380, Edmond Terry's evidence.
38 WO 71/380, Mrs Terry's evidence.
39 WO 71/380, David McGuire's evidence.

Ellen Terry, sister of the accused, was the next witness and stated that she lived in Clonmult with her grandmother, Mrs Ellen Fitzgerald. She confirmed that her brother visited them on 20th February and that she saw John Harty speaking to two others outside at the crossroads. She further stated that when her brother left the house there was another man after joining the group. She didn't know him.[40]

The next witness, Mrs Kate Hennessy, stated that around 12 noon on that Sunday morning, Edmond Terry and John Harty had purchased either two or three packets of cigarettes in her shop. She said she had known both of them for about ten years and they were both very respectable.

Cross-examined by the prosecutor, she stated that she could not remember all the cigarettes that she sold that day and that she had been asked to give evidence in this case eight or ten days ago.

Re-examined by Mr Comyn, she stated that she heard around 24th February that John Harty had been arrested. She stated that when she heard that they had been arrested that she had recalled that they had been in the shop on the 20th.[41]

The sixth witness was Miss Catherine Daly and she stated she was an assistant in her aunt's sweet and cigarette shop in Cloyne. She also stated that on 20th February John Harty and Edmond Terry came into the shop.

Cross-examined by the prosecutor, she stated that the boys bought some Player's cigarettes. Edmond Terry bought two packets. She was asked to give evidence about a week before and she was also asked if she remembered the two boys coming into the shop and if Edmond Terry had bought two packets of cigarettes. She said it was a busy day after mass. She could not remember who exactly purchased what on that day but she did remember speaking to the two boys.

Re-examined by Mr Comyn, she stated that a few days later she heard that the two boys had been arrested and she remembered then that they had been in the shop on the Sunday.[42]

The next examined was the accused, John Harty. He stated that he was 18 years of age, a farmer's son and he lived in Ballyroe, located between Cloyne and Churchtown South. His evidence concurred with that of Edmond Terry, regarding mass, the cigarettes and deciding to go to Clonmult. He also stated that he had to borrow his sister's bicycle for the journey. He stated that they

---

40   WO 71/380, Ellen Terry's evidence.
41   WO 71/380, Mrs Kate Hennessy's evidence.
42   WO 71/380, Miss Catherine Daly's evidence.

met the other two on the way, about meeting Dick Hegarty, whom he knew, and about going to the farmhouse with him. He had the same experience in the farmhouse as Edmond Terry. It was further stated that:

> After the surrender he was the third or fourth out of the house and he was about 25 yards outside the door he was passing between a group of soldiers and police when he was hit on the side of the head by something, he thought it was the butt end of a rifle. He got up again and went over to where seven or eight men were standing beside the wall of the barn. The men standing against the wall with him were Edmond Terry, William Garde and Robert Walsh, he didn't know the others.

He stated that he spent three days in hospital.[43] Under cross-examination he further stated that he was not a member, had never been a member nor had ever been asked to join a Sinn Féin club. He said that he thought there was a Sinn Féin club in Churchtown and that he didn't know if there was one in Cloyne. He also stated that he was not a member and had never been a member of the Irish Volunteers or IRA.

Examined by the court, he stated that when he went into the house there was confusion, three or four running around. The front door led straight into the kitchen. When he came out of the house he was close to the man in front and he didn't know him.[44]

The eighth witness for the defence, Miss Margaret Harty, stated she was the oldest in the family, sister of the accused John Harty and had one other brother. On 20th February, she went to 8.30 am mass in Cloyne, returning home about 10 am. After dinner her brother asked to borrow her bicycle as Edmond Terry had asked him to go to Clonmult. One of them gave her some cigarettes before they left.

Cross-examined by the prosecutor, she stated that her brother often gave her cigarettes and that she often lent him her bicycle, mainly on Sunday afternoons. She did not know the make or number of her bicycle but she would know it again because the carrier was broken.[45]

William Garde was the next accused to be examined. He stated that he was 17½ years of age and lived in Ballynamona, near Ballycotton. He stated that he was not a Sinn Féiner nor a member of any illegal organisation. He also stated

---

43 *Cork Examiner*, 16th March 1921 and WO 71/380, John Harty's evidence.

44 WO 71/380, John Harty's evidence.

45 WO 71/380, Margaret Harty's evidence.

that he slept at home on the night of 19th February and drove his mother to Ballycotton mass, meeting his first cousin, Robert Walsh, there. Afterwards, they had dinner together in Garde's house and then decided to go for a cycle. They left the house around 12.30. They met Edmond Terry and John Harty in Ladysbridge. Edmond Terry said he was going to see his grandmother in Clonmult as she was ill. The two of them decided to go with Harty and Terry. The main part of his evidence was the same as that given by the previous accused. Detailing the events following his surrender, he stated that he was the second out the door and the police and soldiers were in front of him. The shooting started when they were about 25 yards out and he saw the man in front of him fall.

> I had my hands up when I was shot, the man in front had his hands up until he fell. I heard six or seven shots and they came from the direction from where the police were standing. The police had revolvers in their hands and I saw smoke coming from them. The first shot I heard after coming out of the house was the shot that hit the man in front of me. I think the second shot hit me. We were then taken prisoner, searched and marched across the fields to the lorries and from there to Cork.[46]

Cross-examined by the prosecutor, he said he was surprised to see Dick Hegarty at Clonmult. He didn't know if he was working in Clonmult, he might have been 'on the run', he didn't know. After surrendering he was searched up against the outside wall of the cowshed and taken inside afterwards. Edmond Terry, John Harty and Robert Walsh were with him all the time.[47]

The tenth witness on Wednesday, 16th March, was Robert Garde, farmer and father of the accused, William Garde. He confirmed that William was 17 and that he had two brothers and two sisters. He said William had left school about two years previously and had been following horses and doing some farm work. He also stated that the accused Robert Walsh was William's first cousin. His evidence corresponded with the details given as evidence by his son of the events of the Sunday morning. He said that he knew Sgt Donaldson of the RIC in his district and he had known him for eight years. He stated that there were no firearms in his house and that his son had no firearms.

---

46   *Cork Examiner*, 16th March 1921 and WO 71/380.
47   WO 71/380, William Garde's evidence.

Cross-examined by the prosecutor, he stated that his son never told him anything about what he proposed to do on Sunday, 20th February.[48]

The eleventh witness was Mrs Mary Garde and she stated that she was the mother of the accused, William Garde. Her evidence regarding the Sunday morning was as given by her son and husband. She further stated that her son was not in any illegal organisation and that there were no firearms in her house.

Cross-examined by the prosecutor, she stated that she knew that any illegal organisation is anything against His Majesty. She also stated that her son, William, and his friend, Robert Walsh, had dinner together in her house before setting off that day.

Examined by the court, she stated that she heard on Tuesday, the 22nd, that William had been arrested. When he hadn't returned by 6 o'clock on the Sunday evening she became very uneasy.[49]

The accused Robert Walsh was next to be examined and he stated that he was just over 20 years of age, he lived in Ballycotton and his father was dead and his mother was a farmer. His evidence of the events of that Sunday morning was the same as given by William Garde. He stated that in 1915 during the Great War, aged 15, he had joined the Royal Munster Fusiliers and was discharged as under age. In 1916, aged 16, he had enlisted in the 3rd Battalion of the Leinster Regiment and shortly afterwards was transferred to the Royal Irish Regiment, but had been discharged again as under age. His evidence for the events at Clonmult was the same as given by the previous defendants. He also stated that the accused Edmond Terry, after being shot, fell down beside him and was lying on the ground for a good spell. He stated that he was not and had never been a member of any illegal organisation but that he had been in the British Army.

Cross-examined, he stated that he had borrowed the bicycle from a Mrs Roche and that it was a lady's. He had never been to Clonmult before and he didn't know that Edmond Terry had a grandmother there. He gave details of the events in the house and in the yard as already detailed elsewhere.[50]

Mrs Bridget Walsh, Robert Walsh's mother, was the thirteenth witness to be examined and she provided a character witness for her son. She confirmed that he had enlisted twice in the British Army. She had expected him home around 6 o'clock on the Sunday evening and was disappointed when he did not arrive.

---

48   WO 71/380, Robert Garde's evidence.

49   WO 71/380, Mrs Mary Garde's evidence.

50   *Cork Examiner*, 17th March 1921 and WO 71/380, Roberts Walsh's evidence.

She received a letter from him on the following Tuesday morning from the Detention Barracks.[51]

A letter was produced by Mr Comyn, from RIC Sergeant Donaldson, in which Robert Walsh and William Garde were given excellent character references. This closed the evidence in the cases of the accused for which Mr Comyn appeared.

Mr McCarthy, B.L., counsel for the accused Maurice Moore, Patrick O'Sullivan and Jeremiah (Diarmuid) O'Leary, opened with a character reference for O'Sullivan.

The accused Patrick O'Sullivan stated that he was 24 years of age and lived in Queenstown with his mother. He said he had two brothers in the British Army and a brother killed in the Royal Navy on HMS 'Hawke'.[52] His mother had a pension in respect of his death. He stated that he joined a Sinn Féin club last summer and was not a member of any other branch of the organisation. In the Sinn Féin club he was the assistant secretary of an arbitration court. He had been requested to join the Irish Volunteers but he had refused. O'Sullivan gave evidence that he himself was on the run from the IRA and was in fact a prisoner at Clonmult. He admitted to being a member of Sinn Féin but that he was not a Volunteer. He admitted being the acting secretary of the Sinn Féin Arbitration Court in Queenstown and that he organised the courts to be held in the Town Hall in Queenstown. After the court was raided by the military, he stated he had to go on the run from the IRA because it was believed that he had given the details of the court to the police and because the military had raided his house. He went to Carrigtwohill and while there met a man named Barry from Lisgoold. He gave him employment and he remained with him for about a month. He left when a threshing machine arrived and followed the machine around until last December. After that, using the name Paddy Maher, he worked for about six weeks for a Mr O'Riordan, also from Lisgoold. He then travelled around the area looking for work until he ended up in a public house in Clonmult.[53]

His story was that he was in the public house on the Friday prior to the battle when a stranger offered him work. They met the following day and he followed the man a short distance to a farmhouse. On the way they met five or six other men and they insisted that he should have been blindfolded, which he

---

51   *Cork Examiner*, 17th March 1921 and WO 71/380, Mrs Bridget Walsh's evidence.

52   *A Great Sacrifice, Cork Servicemen Who Died in the Great War*, p. 456, Sullivan, Bartholomew, 9 Thomas Street, Queenstown (Cobh), died at sea, 15 October 1914, aged 24.

53   WO 71/380, Patrick O'Sullivan's evidence.

immediately was. Then he was brought to the farmhouse as a prisoner, taken up to the loft and handcuffed. The kitchen was inside the front door and he saw two other rooms downstairs in the house. The loft was above the kitchen. He remained there until the military arrived on Sunday, 20th February. He remained handcuffed in the loft until after the roof was set on fire, then the fumes drove him downstairs. When he came down he saw the accused Jeremiah O'Leary lying wounded in a bed. He brought O'Leary out and both ended up in the shed, where they were searched. He heard a lot of commotion going on outside and he heard a British officer shout 'to draw the police off'. He was later searched, taken to the lorries, and later taken to Cork. While being searched and later on the journey to Cork, he told a military sergeant that he had been held as a prisoner in Clonmult. He stated next that his brother, an ex-soldier, was working in Admiralty House, Queenstown, under his own name and that he himself worked as a clerk in Haulbowline.[54]

Cross-examined by the prosecutor and in his defence, he swore that he was not a section commander of the IRA. He was questioned about his position in the Arbitration Court and in evidence he admitted that a court document shown as evidence was sent out by the accused. He repeated that he was on the run from Sinn Féin and not the military. He was also questioned as to why he was able to work so close to home while claiming to be on the run from the IRA. To this he replied that he was not using his own name and the people didn't know him. He then appeared to suggest that there was another Patrick O'Sullivan in Queenstown who was involved in the Irish Volunteers, but that he was not that man. He repeated that until the military arrived he was kept handcuffed, blindfolded and a close prisoner.[55]

The fifteenth witness, Thomas Riordan, stated that he was a farmer from Lisgoold and that he recognised the accused Pat O'Sullivan as Paddy Maher. He had employed him late last year, until three armed and masked men called to him while in the field. They said they came as members of the IRA and that there was a man in his employ that was suspected. He paid him off immediately. The next contact he had with the accused was a letter from the Detention Barracks.

Cross-examined by the prosecutor, he stated that his farm was called Lisgoold West and it was 199 acres and in his brother, John's, name. The accused said he would be able to feed cattle and was not asked about his previous experience. The witness did not report the three armed and masked men to the police.

---

54   *Cork Examiner*, 17th March 1921.
55   WO 71/380 and Patrick O'Sullivan's evidence.

Maher was working about the yard when they came and they did not ask to see him. There was nothing preventing them from taking Maher away. When Maher left, the witness never saw him again until here in court.[56]

The accused Maurice Moore was next examined. He stated that he was 25 years of age and lived in a labourer's cottage outside Queenstown with his father and five brothers. During the war he worked in Haulbowline for five years as a dockyard labourer. He slept at home on 19th February. On the morning of the battle he decided to cycle to Carrigtwohill and on to Midleton. He met James Ahern and James Glavin in Midleton and Ahern told him that Patrick O'Sullivan was a prisoner in Clonmult, and that he was to go out to identify him. He agreed to cycle to Clonmult with them. The three were at the farmhouse solely for the purpose of identifying O'Sullivan. James Ahern went into the loft to identify O'Sullivan and Moore went into the kitchen, where he met and spoke to David Desmond and Jeremiah Ahern. James Ahern came down and confirmed that O'Sullivan was the prisoner. A few minutes later there was a shout because the British troops had suddenly arrived and as a result they were trapped inside. After the surrender, he was taken by one of the British officers to identify some of the bodies. He identified Glavin, who was lying dead alongside the wall of the barn. He identified Jeremiah Ahern, who was lying dead in a field about 100 yards from the house. He saw Desmond lying dead at the back of the house.[57] He admitted to being a member of the IRA, Sinn Féin and the Fianna but swore he was not a member of the militant wing of any of them and had never had anything to do with firearms.

Cross-examined by the prosecutor, he stated that the IRA and the Irish Volunteers were the same and that he was a section commander of number three section of the Queenstown Company of 4th Battalion. He knew all the other section commanders and that none of the accused were among them. As a section leader he did nothing but drilling men and used no arms in connection with that.

Examined by the court, he stated he was a member of the three illegal organisations that he mentioned and had never been in the house before.[58]

The next witness to be examined, the seventeenth, was Michael Moore, father of Maurice, and he stated that he lived in Queenstown and that his son

---

56   WO 71/380 and Thomas Riordan's evidence.
57   *Cork Examiner*, 19th March 1921.
58   WO 71/380, Maurice Moore's evidence.

slept at home on Saturday night, 19th February. He left home between 10 and 11 o'clock the following morning. He was not cross-examined.[59]

The last of the accused to be examined, Jeremiah (Diarmuid) O'Leary, stated that he was not yet 20 years old and that he was the only surviving son of his widowed mother. He had one sister and that two of his brothers had died at home from injuries received in the Great War.[60] He too slept at home on Saturday, 19th February, and after mass in Ballymacoda on Sunday morning he met a man named Daniel Murphy. He next met a girl called Rosie McCarthy and she asked him to take a parcel to Clonmult to a man named Dick Hegarty, whom he knew well. He cycled to Clonmult and when he reached the village he saw Hegarty in the distance with four others. He followed them and left his bicycle where the road turns right towards the farmhouse. He did not catch up with them until they reached the farmhouse. He gave the parcel to Hegarty, it had spare clothes in it. He just happened to reach the house a few minutes before the military arrived, therefore, he too was trapped inside. He went into a small room and he threw himself on top of a bed. The room was to the left of the kitchen and was about eight or nine feet square with a window facing out front. The shooting began and after three or four shots were fired, a dog jumped on top of him. Raising himself suddenly, being afraid that the dog would bite him, he was wounded by a bullet in the head. He could not remember anything afterwards. The next he remembered was going into hospital.[61] He stated that he had no politics and was not a member of Sinn Féin, the Irish Volunteers or the IRA. He further stated that he had met Hegarty about two months before in Ballymacoda and that he didn't know where he lived.

Cross-examined by the prosecutor, he stated that Ballymacoda was in the direction of the sea from Killeagh and away from Clonmult. The lady did not say how she came to have the clothing. She lived between Ladysbridge and Ballymacoda.[62]

The nineteenth witness, Rosie McCarthy, the young girl mentioned by O'Leary, stated that she gave the parcel of clothes for Hegarty to O'Leary, in Ballymacoda, on the Sunday morning. She knew that Hegarty was in Clonmult but she did not know exactly where. She had bought the clothes herself.

---

59   *Ibid.*

60   No O'Leary from Killeagh found on the register of Cork, Great War dead.

61   *Cork Examiner*, 19th March 1921 and WO 71/380, Jeremiah (Diarmuid) O'Leary's evidence.

62   WO 71/380, Jeremiah (Diarmuid) O'Leary's evidence.

Questioned by the court, she stated that she knew that Hegarty was on the run.[63]

The next witness, Daniel Murphy, stated that he met O'Leary in Ballymacoda on the Sunday after mass and that O'Leary told him that he was on his way to Clonmult.[64]

Witness Edward Wallace stated that he knew the accused, O'Leary, and he last saw him in Mogeely, on the road to Clonmult, on Sunday, 20th February.

Cross-examined by the prosecutor, he stated that he met him on the north side of Mogeely and he was on his way to Clonmult, but that he didn't know the road or how far it was. He also stated that he was not asked to give evidence in this case but about two weeks ago he volunteered to do so.[65]

On Saturday, 19th March, the trial concluded with the closing addresses given by Mr Comyn and Mr McCarthy.

On behalf of the men they represented, Mr Comyn, K.C., pointed out that the charge was High Treason and again said that names of witnesses should have been given ten days before the trial. He said his four clients were not members of any illegal organisation and the prosecution was unable to disprove that. He also said that the first shots were fired by the military. Their defence was that the accused came out with their hands up upon surrendering, that the terms of surrender were that they should not be shot, and he appealed for mercy to the accused.

Mr McCarthy stated that bare conspiracy was not an act of levying war and that O'Sullivan, kept in the house by force, could not be guilty of charge. He added that the action of the men in the house was resistance to arrest and not levying war, that O'Sullivan's statement to the military sergeant had not been rebutted, and that proclamation was not proved.

The prosecutor replied, drawing attention to the allegations made by the accused of ill treatment by Crown Forces and that these were contradicted by the accused themselves. He pointed out discrepancies in evidence and that the charge was not High Treason.

The Judge Advocate summed up, pointing out that the charge was not the civil offence of High Treason. He directed the court that unless it was proved that the accused took part in or aided and abetted with others in an armed attack they must be acquitted.[66]

---

63 WO 71/380, Rosie McCarthy's evidence.
64 WO 71/380, Daniel Murphy's evidence.
65 WO 71/380, Edward Wallace's evidence.
66 UKNA, Clonmult WO 71/380.

Proceeding after findings:[67]

Mr Comyn handed in a letter as to the character of Robert Garde.
Mr McCarthy handed in a letter as to the character of Pat Sullivan.
All the accused declined to address the court or to say anything further.
The court was adjourned to consider sentence.

The court retired for twenty minutes before returning guilty verdicts in respect of all of the men.[68]

On Monday, 21st March, a detailed transcript of the entire court proceedings was sent by Maj-Gen Strickland in Victoria Barracks to General Headquarters in Dublin. Included in the file was the following letter:[69]

GHQ   L/410
Ireland,
Herewith proceedings of a Military Court in the Clonmult Case.
The accused Jeremiah O'Leary denied he was a member of any illegal association, and nothing is known against him here. He states that he lost two brothers in the war.

He was aware that there were rebels in the party at Clonmult when he went there, but there is some doubt whether he was a member of the gang, and under the circumstances it is recommended that clemency be exercised in his case. A full newspaper account of this case is enclosed.

HQ, 6Div   Signed: E.P. Strickland
Cork, 21.3.21   Major Gen, Commanding 6th Division[70]

The evidence given by the four accused, John Harty, William Garde, Robert Walsh and Edmond Terry, was only partially accurate. It is quite understandable that they did not volunteer the fact that the cigarettes that Terry bought were for the members of the column and not for his grandmother. The principal reason for Harty and Terry going to Clonmult was to deliver money that had been collected from the farmers in their area for the IRA. As well as being the column headquarters, it was a collecting point for these funds. The evidence

---

67   *Ibid.*
68   Sean Enright, *The Trial of Civilians by Military Courts Ireland 1921*, p. 85.
69   UK NA, Clonmult Military Court case file, WO 71/380.
70   WO 71/380.

given by the three accused, Patrick O'Sullivan, Maurice Moore and Diarmuid (Jeremiah) O'Leary, could not have been further from the truth. They were all active IRA men and were fully involved in the column. The truth would have convicted all three.

During the course of the Military Court, the legal team for the accused made an attempt to halt the proceedings on a number of legal issues. These issues formed the basis for an appeal to a higher civil court in Dublin in the aftermath of the trial. On the Tuesday following the conclusion of the Military Court, it was announced that three of the prisoners, O'Sullivan, Moore and O'Leary, were sentenced to death and were to be executed by firing squad. All executions in the Martial Law areas were by firing squads. In the remainder of the country, outside the Martial Law area, executions were by hanging as captured Republicans were tried under Civil Law. The fate of the other four was not immediately known. Later their sentence was announced. The four youths were sentenced to penal servitude for life. An appeal was immediately lodged and a temporary order was granted by the King's Bench Division of the High Court in Dublin on 23rd March. This prevented the military authorities in Cork from carrying out the death sentences imposed on three of the seven men pending a full appeal being heard. Letters were sent by the members of Midleton U.D.C. to the Prime Minister in Downing St, and to the Chief Secretary's Office in Dublin, appealing for the lives of the three men.

The appeal was heard in Dublin on the 20th and 21st April 1921 and was listed as 'The King (Garde and Others) v. MAJOR-GENERAL E. P. STRICKLAND and Others'.[71] The appeal was heard before Chief Justice C.J. Moloney and judges Dodd, Pim, Gordon and J.J. Samuels. The men were represented by Michael Comyn, K.C., and Sgt MacSwiney, K.C. The Crown was represented by Sergeant Hanna, K.C., who had appeared for the Crown in the case of Allen.[72]

The order was applied for on the grounds:[73]

1. That the Military Court had no jurisdiction to try the prisoners.
2. That no state of war existed sufficiently to justify the existence of Martial Law or a court established in pursuance thereof.

---

71   T. Henry Maxwell, *The Irish Reports, 1921, Vol. 2, The King's Bench Division*,
      The Incorporated Council of Law Reporting for Ireland, Dublin, 1921, p. 317.
72   Sean Enright, *The Trial of Civilians by Military Courts Ireland 1921*, p. 87.
73   T. Henry Maxwell, *The Irish Reports, 1921, Vol. 2, The King's Bench Division*, p. 317.

3. That the names, professions, and places of abode of the witnesses for the prosecution were not given according to law or at all.
4. That the names of the members of the Military Court were not given.
5. That the said William Garde, John Harty, Edmond Terry, Maurice Moore, Robert Walsh, Pat Sullivan, and Jeremiah O'Leary were indicted and tried without the oath of two lawful witnesses to an overt act of treason.

The appeal hinged on whether or not a state of war existed in Cork. If a state of war did exist, then the authorities were deemed as correct in declaring the region as a Martial Law area and consequently, persons captured under arms could be tried by Military Court.

Affidavits were presented from prominent citizens of Cork, declaring that 'normal life, entertainment and business life of the city and county daily continued and that the courts were still sitting'. In reply, an affidavit was sworn by Gen Macready that 'a state of open rebellion existed, amounting to actual warfare of a guerrilla character, and that ordinary life was carried on due to the presence of large numbers of Crown Forces'.[74] Gen Macready also listed the casualty figures for the Crown Forces in the Martial Law areas to prove his submission that a state of war did exist.[75] Precedence had been set in a previous appeal, Rex *v.* Allen, February 1921, where it was conceded that a state of war did exist.[76] The appeal finished on 21st April, and the judgement was delivered to the court by the Lord Chief Justice on 25th April.[77]

Giving his judgement, the Lord Chief Justice briefly recounted the events that led to the trial, the background to the introduction of Martial Law, and the grounds on which the appeal was made. He went on:

> In the case of The King v. Allen in which I delivered the judgement of the Court on the 24th of February last, we were unanimously of the opinion, that there was at that date a state of war in the area included in the Lord Lieutenant's proclamation justifying the application of Martial Law, and the only question which arises for decision in the present case is as to whether that state of war still continues.[78]

---

74   *The Irish Reports, 1921, Vol. 2, The King's Bench Division*, pp. 319–320. (UCC Q+2).
75   *Ibid.* p. 329.
76   *Ibid.* p. 325.
77   *The Irish Reports, 1921, Vol. 2, The King's Bench Division*, p. 327.
78   *The Irish Reports, 1921, Vol. 2, The King's Bench Division*, pp. 328–329.

The affidavit sworn by Gen Macready highlighting the Crown Forces' casualties in the Martial Law area was sufficient to convince the appeal judges that the state of war did indeed still exist. In his affidavit to the Allen appeal, Gen Macready had sworn that between 1st June 1920 and 10th February 1921, six military officers, twenty-four other ranks and sixty-two members of the police had been murdered. In his affidavit for this appeal, the figures of fatalities among Crown Forces up to 10th April 1921 had increased to fourteen officers, fifty-four other ranks and 101 police.[79]

The Lord Chief Justice concluded the judgement: 'The attempt to distinguish this case from Allen's Case therefore fails on all grounds, and we must discharge the conditional order.'[80]

Having failed in the legal appeal, the local representatives in Cork City and in East Cork opened a petition on the 26th, which was signed by the families, friends and supporters of the three condemned men. The petition books were available in the city, the Town Halls in Midleton and Cobh and in the Carnegie Library in Killeagh.[81] The petitions were to be sent to the Lord Lieutenant in Dublin. This was the last chance to save the three IRA men. The lives of Patrick O'Sullivan, Maurice Moore and Diarmuid O'Leary were hanging by a thread.

---

79   *Ibid*. pp. 329–330.
80   *Ibid*. p. 332.
81   *Cork Examiner*, 27th April 1921.

THE EXECUTIONS

The eight weeks between 28th January and 23rd March 1921 were particularly costly in terms of lives lost for the IRA in County Cork:

On 28th January at Dripsey, an IRA ambushing party was taken by surprise by British troops, after the location of the ambush was reported to the authorities by a local Loyalist, Mrs Mary Lindsay. Seven IRA men and three civilians were taken prisoner. One of the captured IRA men later died of his wounds. The six others were subsequently tried by Military Court and five were executed in the Cork Military Detention Barracks on 28th February. The three civilians were released.[1]

On 15th February, at Mourne Abbey, south of Mallow, in Liam Lynch's 2nd Brigade area, an ambushing party was also taken by surprise. In the battle, four of the IRA men died and eight were taken prisoner, of whom two, Thomas Mulcahy and Patrick Ronayne, were later executed in the Cork Military Detention Barracks on 28th April alongside two of the men captured at Clonmult.[2]

On the same day, in the 3rd Brigade area, three IRA men and six civilians were killed, during a failed ambush on British soldiers travelling on a civilian train at Upton railway station.[3]

---

1   P.J. Feeney, *Glory O, Glory O, Ye Bold Fenian Men*, p. 156.
2   Florence O'Donoghue, *No Other Law*, pp. 137–138.
3   Tom Barry, *Guerrilla Days in Ireland*, p. 93.

Two days later, on 17th February, the Thursday before Clonmult, in west Cork, four IRA men were taken by surprise and killed while cutting a trench across a road near Kilbrittain, five miles south of Bandon.

The following Sunday, the Battle of Clonmult took place, resulting in twelve IRA dead and eight captured.

On 23rd March, seven IRA men were asleep in a shed at Clogheen on the western outskirts of Cork City, without sentries being posted. Their location was passed on to the British, who immediately raided the building. Six of the men were shot dead.[4]

A factor common in five of the six reversals mentioned above was a lack of early warning. The importance of sentries was still not fully appreciated. Following the engagements at Dripsey, Mourne Abbey and Clonmult, the British had a total of twenty-four prisoners.

In the aftermath of these reversals, the IRA did not immediately seek revenge for their losses. However, on 17th February, following the Dripsey ambush, the IRA kidnapped Mrs Mary Lindsay and her chauffeur, James Clarke, because she had informed the British military of the ambush.[5] When, following their trials, five of the IRA men were sentenced to be executed, the military authorities were told by the IRA that the hostages would only be released in exchange for the lives of the IRA men. The five from Dripsey and a sixth from Tipperary were executed in the Military Detention Barracks on 28th February 1921 and Mary Lindsay and James Clarke were shot dead by the IRA shortly afterwards.

On the night of the executions, the Officer Commanding 1st Brigade IRA, Sean O'Hegarty, unleashed his men. Between 6.30 pm and 8 pm gunfire was heard all over the city. The result was that the Active Service Unit in Cork City under Pa Murray shot dead six British soldiers and a further four were wounded.[6] This was the pattern set in the aftermath of Clonmult; no immediate reprisals, an attempt to take a prominent person hostage and unleash the gunmen only if all else failed.

Following the trials of the Clonmult and Mourne Abbey prisoners, the instruction was issued by IRA Brigade headquarters in Cork to attempt to kidnap a senior British Army officer. Shortly afterwards, IRA men under

---

4   P.J. Feeney, *Glory O, Glory O, Ye Bold Fenian Men*, p. 156.
5   Sean O'Callaghan, *Execution*, p. 144.
6   *Ibid.* p. 161.

Frank Busteed kidnapped Maj G.L. Compton-Smith of the Royal Welch Fusiliers; he was the officer in charge of Ballyvonaire Camp, located between Buttevant and Mallow.[7] He had travelled alone on the train from Buttevant on 16th April and had left the train at Blarney to walk the short distance to Smith's hotel in the village.[8] A dispatch was sent to Gen Strickland informing him that Maj Compton-Smith was a prisoner of the IRA and was being held in exchange for the lives of the men who were under sentence of death, following Clonmult and Mourne Abbey.[9] He was held in safe houses in the vicinity of Donoughmore, in mid-Cork. During his time in captivity, he was allowed to write to his wife, Gladys, in England. Despite widespread searches by the British forces in the area, he remained in IRA hands. His fate would be determined later.

In the weeks between the Battle of Clonmult and the executions of Patrick O'Sullivan and Maurice Moore, there were very few incidents in the 4th Battalion area. This was primarily because most of the men who had been active were either dead or captured. However, on Sunday, 10th April, Diarmuid O'Hurley, Joseph Ahern, Paddy Whelan and other activists attempted to blow up a British Army convoy as it passed Ballyedikin junction, three miles east of Midleton, on the road to Youghal.[10] They also placed a bomb against the front wall of the courthouse in Midleton in the early hours of the following morning, causing considerable damage.

The day before the executions, Jeremiah O'Leary was in the exercise yard of the Military Detention Barracks with Patrick O'Sullivan and Maurice Moore when he was called for a visit. His mother and sister were waiting to see him. When the visit was over, he went back to the exercise yard to find that his two comrades had been removed to their cells. What had happened in the interim was that orders had been received by the prison authorities that the two men were to be executed the following morning. The condemned men, two for Clonmult and two for Mourne Abbey, Thomas Mulcahy and Patrick Ronayne, were confined to their cells until the following morning. A black cross was pinned to their cell doors and sentries were placed outside their cells.

On the eve of his execution, Vol Patrick O'Sullivan penned his last letter to his elderly mother in Cobh:[11]

---

7   Tim Sheehan, *Execute Hostage Compton-Smith*, p. 79.

8   P.J. Feeney, *Glory O, Glory O, Ye Bold Fenian Men*, p. 157.

9   Tim Sheehan, *Execute Hostage Compton-Smith*, p. 86.

10   *Rebel Cork's Fighting Story*, p. 195.

11   *Rebel Cork's Fighting Story*, (Kerryman edition only), p. 157, also, *Cork Examiner*, 6th May 1921.

MILITARY BARRACKS, CORK.

27th of April, 1921.

MY DEAREST MOTHER,

I sincerely hope and trust that God and His Blessed Virgin Mother Mary will comfort and console you and enable yourself and poor father to bear this trial with patience and to suffer all for the holy Will of God, also my loving brothers, relations and friends.

I am in great spirits and pray for the hour to come when I will be released from this world of sorrow and suffering. We must all die some day, and I am simply going by an early train. Jesus and Mary were my friends and supports in all the trials of life, and now that death is coming they are truer and better friends than ever.

You can be rest assured that I will be happy in Heaven, and although I have to leave you in mourning, you will be consoled to think that I am going to meet God in Heaven and also my brothers and sister. Why should I fear to die, when death will only unite me to God in Heaven. If I could choose my own death, I would not ask to die otherwise. In fact I am delighted to have had such a glorious opportunity of gaining eternal salvation as well as serving my country. My death will help with the others, and remember that those who die for Ireland never die.

Don't let my death cause you too much unnecessary worry or grief, and then when I get to Heaven I will constantly pray to God for the kind and loving parents He gave me, to help them to bear this little Cross. Tell my loving brothers and friends that I will also remember them.

Good-bye now, my dearest and best of mothers, until we meet again in Heaven and God.

Your fond and loving son,

Paddy.

That night, Jeremiah O'Leary received a visit from a priest, who told him he was to be shot in the morning. Later, a soldier who brought him tea, told him, 'They are keeping you for your mate in hospital.' O'Leary recalled, 'Apparently we were to be shot in pairs. I need scarcely say I did not have much sleep that night.'[12]

---

12   Diarmuid (Jeremiah) O'Leary, *WS No. 1589*, p. 11.

On Thursday, 28th April 1921, four men were executed in the Military Detention Barracks in Cork, the recently closed Cork Prison. Thomas Mulcahy (18) and Patrick Ronayne (24), having being captured at Mourne Abbey, were executed at 8.05 am. Patrick O'Sullivan (22) and Maurice Moore (24), both from Cobh, for their involvement at Clonmult, were executed at 8.15 am. The men received their last visitors on the previous day.

A handwritten note in pencil in the Military Court case file sums it up:

The executions took place this morning at Cork of:

Patrick Ronayne	Mourne
Thos. Mulcahy	Mourne
Pat Sullivan	Clonmult[13]
Maurice Moore	Clonmult[14]

Who were tried for taking part in armed insurrection and being involved in ambushes against Forces of the Crown. They were found guilty and sentenced to death.[15]

Very Rev Canon O'Sullivan and Rev W. O'Brien, C.C. were with the prisoners at an early hour in the morning. At 7 o'clock they assisted at mass celebrated by Father O'Brien and received Holy Communion. At 7.30 am Canon O'Sullivan said mass and the prisoners were joined in their prayers by Rev Father O'Brien.[16]

After the masses in the oratory, the prisoners were removed to their cells, and within a few minutes, accompanied by the Rev Canon O'Sullivan and Fr O'Brien, were marched to the place of execution in pairs. When the firing party discharged the volley, they withdrew and the priests then went to the dead men and anointed them and imparted Papal Benediction. The prisoners met their death with firmness and fortitude.[17]

---

13   UKNA, Kew, Military Court of Inquiry in Lieu of Inquest, Patrick O'Sullivan, WO 35/159B/16.
14   UKNA, Kew, Military Court of Inquiry in Lieu of Inquest, Maurice Moore, WO 35/155B/18.
15   UKNA Kew, Clonmult Military Court case file, WO 71/380.
16   Canon O'Sullivan was diocesan administrator and Father O'Brien was the prison chaplain and also curate in the North Cathedral, see, Sean O'Callaghan, *Execution*, pp. 153–154.
17   *Cork Examiner*, 29th April 1921.

Immediately after the executions, the bodies were examined by Maj O.C.F. Cooke, Royal Army Medical Corps. In all four cases death was found to be instantaneous. Maj Peter Trant-Foley, O.B.E., Assistant Provost Marshal, 6th Division, supervised all four executions.[18]

On the same day as the executions, a 'Military Court of Inquiry in Lieu of an Inquest' was held in Victoria Barracks. The death certificates signed on the day of the executions state that death was caused by shock and haemorrhage due to rifle fire in execution of the sentence of a Military Court.[19]

Following the executions, the four bodies were transported by military ambulance to the Cork Male Gaol off Western Road and now part of UCC. Under the supervision of Lt A.C.O. Greenwood, officer in charge of the Burial Working Party, the four bodies were buried at 9 o'clock that morning.[20] Applications made by their families to the military authorities for the return of the bodies were refused. The bodies remain buried there to this day. On the morning of the executions, at 11 o'clock in St Colman's Cathedral in Cobh, a solemn requiem mass was said for the repose of the souls of the two natives of that town. The mass was celebrated by Rev D. O'Keeffe. All the shops in the town were closed. At Rushbrook Convent Chapel, early morning mass was celebrated by Rev P. Fouhy for the same purpose.[21]

On the evening of the executions, Jeremiah O'Leary was taken to an office in the barracks, where three British Army officers were present. He recalled, 'One of them proceeded to read out the sentence of death passed on me and then added that the sentence was commuted to one of Penal Servitude for Life. It is not possible to state the relief I felt at this totally unexpected news.'[22]

O'Leary had been found guilty of levying war and sentenced to death. During his court martial he denied having any involvement whatsoever with the Republican forces. He also claimed that two of his brothers were killed while serving with the British forces during the First World War. His strategy proved successful in the end. In an amazing twist, the General Officer Commanding the 6th Division in Victoria Barracks, Cork, Maj-Gen E.P. Strickland personally intervened, as can be seen in the letter reproduced on page 85.

---

18   UKNA, WO 71/386.
19   UKNA, Clonmult file, WO 71/380.
20   UKNA, WO 71/386.
21   *Cork Examiner*, 29th April 1921.
22   Diarmuid O'Leary, *WS No. 1589*, p. 11.

On Friday, the 29th, it was officially announced that the five remaining Clonmult prisoners had been reprieved.[23] Having been found guilty at the conclusion of their trial, four of the accused – John Harty, Edmond Terry, William Garde and Robert Walsh – were all sentenced to penal servitude for life. Paddy Higgins was still awaiting his trial, which eventually opened in Victoria Barracks on Monday, 21st June 1921.

---

23   *Cork Examiner*, 30th April 1921.

THE IRA AND CROWN FORCES REPRISALS

On 29th April, the day after the executions, Maj Compton-Smith was informed by an unnamed IRA Brigade officer, who was accompanied by the C.O. of the Sixth Battalion, Jackie O'Leary, that he was to be shot. He was given one hour to prepare for his execution. He made two last requests. Firstly, he wished to write a last letter to his wife and secondly, he requested 'the benefit of spiritual consolation from a clergyman' before he died. His first request was granted, but, as there was no Protestant clergyman in the vicinity of Donoughmore, his second request was refused.[1] Before entering the shed where Maj Compton-Smith was held captive, Jackie O'Leary gave instructions to a few men about digging a grave. Inside he gave a pen and paper to the prisoner, who wrote:

> I am to be shot in an hour's time. Dearest, your hubby will die with your name on his lips, your face before my eyes, and he will die like an Englishman and a soldier. I cannot tell you, sweetheart, how much it means to me to leave you alone. I have only the dearest love for you and my sweet little daughter, Annie. I leave my cigarette case to my regiment, my miniature medals to my father, and my watch to the officer who is about to execute me, because I believe him to be a gentleman and to mark the fact that I bear no malice for carrying out what he sincerely believes to be his duty.
>
> Tender, tender farewell and kisses; Your Own, 'Jack'.[2]

---

1   Tim Sheehan, *Execute Hostage Compton-Smith*, pp. 107–109.
2   *Ibid*. p. 108.

Before he was led out, he requested some warm water to 'wash my body before I return it to the Lord'. Afterwards he prayed as he was led across two fields:[3]

Now the labourer' task is o'er,
Now the battle day is past,
Now upon the farther shore,
Lands the voyager at last.

At the end of the field was a freshly dug grave. He turned to look at the grave and, following a short prayer, he faced the firing squad. Jackie O'Leary gave the orders, 'Aim at the target.' Before he ordered 'Fire,' Compton-Smith was heard to say, 'I love you Gladys.'[4]

Maj Compton-Smith's body remained in that grave until handed over to the Gardaí in late 1924. He was re-interred in Fort Davis, Whitegate, County Cork, in 1925.

After the executions, the IRA was bent on revenge. After Clonmult every suspected informer and every man in uniform, including coastguards and marines, became a legitimate target to be 'shot on sight' in the IRA's quest for vengeance.[5]

On Saturday night, 30th April, ex-soldier Michael O'Keeffe was the target of an IRA snatch squad in the village of Carrigtwohill. The following morning, his body was found with an IRA label attached, declaring him to be a convicted spy. The body was removed to his home.[6]

To quote the C.O. of the 4th Battalion, Mick Leahy:

I sent Dathaí O'Brien to pick up [Michael] O'Keeffe[7] there [in Carrigtwohill] for we had the goods on him. I told him to go down and get this man. O'Brien arrived back in an old Ford car. 'He's in Patsy Connors,' he said. 'But I told you to bring him back here.' 'I know that,' O'Brien said, 'He's on the sidewalk outside and we couldn't bring him back because he's dead. We

3   *Ibid.* p. 110.
4   Tim Sheehan, *Execute Hostage Compton-Smith,* p. 110.
5   *CI Monthly Report, East Cork May 1921* (CO 904/115) and *Rebel Cork's Fighting Story,*
      p. 197, also Peter Hart, *The IRA & Its Enemies, Violence and Community in Cork,
      1916–1923,* p. 98.
6   UKNA Military Court of Inquiry in lieu of an Inquest, Michael O'Keeffe,
      WO 35/157B/5.
7   52111, Gunner Michael O'Keeffe served in the Royal Artillery during the First World
      War, he is buried in the old graveyard in Carrigtwohill.

went down to his house and when we were passing up the street at Patsy Connors' I turned round and let him have it, for he jumped out of the car.[8]

The killings continued the following day, Sunday, 1st May, when two Black and Tans based in the RIC barracks in Castlemartyr were attacked by armed and masked men in a wood beside the village, six miles east of Midleton.[9] Constable William Albert Smith was shot dead and Constable John F. Webb later died of his wounds.[10] The official reprisals followed swiftly. The licensed premises of Mrs Ellen Cronin, and the house of Michael Fitzgerald, both in the village of Clonmult, were destroyed on 6th May. The furniture and personal effects of Patrick Hegarty and William O'Connell, both residents of Castlemartyr, were also destroyed on the same day.

These destructions were ordered by Colonel Commandant H.W. Higginson, C.B., D.S.O., Commanding 17th Infantry Brigade and Military Governor, on the grounds that their owners were supporters of the armed rebels, and that such armed rebels carried out a murderous attack on two members of the RIC at Castlemartyr on 1st May 1921.[11] The burnings of the two buildings in Clonmult have often been regarded as direct reprisals for the support of the column in Clonmult, however, I have now discovered that they were as reprisals for the killing of the two Black and Tans in Castlemartyr. These were in turn killed as reprisals for the execution of the two IRA men captured for Clonmult.

At about 2.30 am on Sunday, 8th May, three volunteers, William Bransfield, Jack Hayes and Dick Masterson, who worked in Keegan's of Carrigtwohill, were dragged from their homes, also in Carrigtwohill, by a party of disguised Crown Forces. Hayes and Masterson managed to escape but Vol William Bransfield was shot dead.[12] He was about 25 years old and had been employed by the Great Southern and Western Railway Company. He was buried in the Republican plot in Midleton, beside the Clonmult men.[13] William Bransfield's wife was a sister of Michael O'Keeffe's widow. As detailed above, ex-soldier Michael O'Keeffe had been killed by the IRA in Carrigtwohill on 30th April.

8   Peter Hart, *The IRA & Its Enemies*, p. 98.
9   Richard Abbott, *Police Casualties in Ireland 1919–1922*, p. 227.
10   UKNA, Mil Court of Inquiry in Lieu of Inquest, RIC Const Webb, WO 35/160/54.
11   *Cork Examiner*, 9th May 1921.
12   UKNA, Mil Court of Inquiry in Lieu of Inquest, Wm Bransfield, WO 35/146B/12.
13   *Cork Examiner*, 10th May 1921.

On Saturday, 14th May 1921 the Crown Forces in Midleton suffered their bloodiest day of the War of Independence. At about 3 pm, RIC Sergeant Joseph Coleman was having a drink in Buckley's public house and grocer's premises on the Main Street when he was shot dead by a local IRA man, Thomas Riordan. When four policemen arrived on the scene, two of them were sent to get a doctor and a priest to minister to the dying sergeant. They were ambushed at the southern end of the town and the two Black and Tans, Thomas Cormyn, from Cavan, and Harold Thompson, an Australian, were killed.[14] The IRA attacked a second party of police who were sent to the scene and during this engagement a Constable McDonald was slightly wounded.[15] The IRA placed a note on the dead body of Constable Thompson, which read simply, 'revenge for Clonmult etc'. This has since been exaggerated to:

> Revenge for Clonmult, we'll have some more,
> You drove to Clonmult, you'll drive no more.

Also on 14th May, two gunners from the Royal Marine Artillery stationed in the Coastguard Station at East Ferry, Marine Bernard Francis and Marine William Parker, were drinking in a public house in Ballinacurra, just outside Midleton.[16] That evening, while walking back to their station, they were abducted just outside Ballinacurra, in the townland of Loughcarrig, by Volunteers Phil Hyde and Daniel Cashman.[17] The two young Marines had grass stuffed into their mouths before being shot dead. Their bodies were thrown into a local quarry.[18] An order had been received from Brigade Headquarters that all British military personnel in uniform should be shot on sight whether they were armed or not.[19]

During Saturday night, 14th May, a large party of Cameron Highlanders came into Midleton and began raiding houses. Some of these soldiers came across Edward McNamara, who was walking along the railway line towards his home. The military shot and killed him. He had no known Republican background. In the early hours of the following morning, Michael Ahern (brother of Volunteer Jack Ahern), Ballyrichard, Midleton, Richard Barry, Knockgriffin, Midleton and John Ryan, Woodstock, Carrigtwohill, were taken from their houses by

---

14   Richard Abbott, *Police Casualties in Ireland 1919–1922*, p. 238.
15   *Cork Examiner*, 16th May 1921.
16   *Cork Examiner*, 16th May 1921 and *Cork's Revolutionary Dead 1916–1923*, pp. 234–235.
17   Daniel Cashman, *WS No. 1523*, p. 12.
18   *Cork's Revolutionary Dead 1916–1923*, pp. 234–235.
19   Daniel Cashman, *WS No. 1523*, p. 12.

British soldiers from the Cameron Highlanders Regiment. Their bullet-riddled bodies were found the following morning.[20] Two other men from Carrigtwohill, Richard Flynn and his son Timothy, were also taken by the military. Richard Flynn was found shot dead the following morning and his son, who was deaf and unable to speak, was seriously wounded.[21] Ten men, five Crown Forces and five civilians had lost their lives within a small area in a little over twelve hours.

It is an indisputable fact that the British Army mobile patrol that travelled to Clonmult on 20th February 1921 was acting on information received from an informer. The patrol travelled from Midleton to Clonmult using the most covert route, they stopped at Rathorgan Crossroads and deployed immediately for their objective, Carey's dwelling house. The local civilians who went to the crossroads were arrested and warned not to go near one of the tenders. The informer was hidden on board.

Following the battle, the IRA were determined to locate the informer. They believed that the culprit was an ex-serviceman who had been seen trapping rabbits in the area. In the aftermath of Clonmult at least two Irishmen, both of whom had served in the British forces, were killed in Carrigtwohill by the IRA. Michael O'Keeffe an ex-soldier, was shot on Saturday, 30th April, and Daniel O'Callaghan, an ex-sailor, was killed on Tuesday, 21st June.

During May, the IRA in the Watergrasshill–Glenville vicinity, which was in the 'C' Company, 1st Battalion, 2nd Brigade area, arrested David Walsh, an ex-soldier, whom they were convinced was the informer.[22] He was questioned by the officer commanding the Company, who attempted to get a confession from him, initially without success. He was taken to a freshly dug grave, where he was told he would be shot if he did not confess. He was also told that if he did confess he would be exiled to Australia. He eventually made a confession and based on this he was court-martialled. Found guilty of informing on the column at Clonmult, he was duly shot. On 21st May, the adjutant of the 1st Battalion sent a report on the arrest, interrogation and execution of David Walsh to the commanding officer of the 4th Battalion.[23] The following is a transcript of that report:[24]

---

20   *Rebel Cork's Fighting Story*, p. 197.
21   *Cork Examiner*, 16th and 17th May 1921.
22   N.L.I., *O'Donoghue papers*, MS 31, 207 (2).
23   UKNA London, CO 904/168, also, B. Ashe, *The Development of the IRA's Concepts of Guerrilla Warfare, 1917–1921*, (U.C.C., 1996), also, N.L.I., *O'Donoghue Papers*, MS 31, 207 (2).
24   NLI, *O'Donoghue papers*, MS 31, 207 (2).

'A' Headquarters Bn, Cork No. 2 Brigade, 21. 5. 1921.

To the O/C 4th Bn, Cork No. 1. Brigade,

1. Yours to hand on 20th inst.
2. The following will be of interest to you. The report re this spy has been filed away, so what I am writing is from memory.
3. Our 'C' Coy Capt arrested a suspicious person of the tramp class and detained him on suspicion for two days.[25] During this time he could get no information from him beyond the fact that he was David Walsh of Shanagarry, and that he was looking for work in Glenville. To extract information from him, the Capt brought him the local C.C. one evening and next morning had a grave made away on the mountains. Here he brought the prisoner, and informed him he was to be shot, and the only way he had of saving his life was by giving full information re himself and his accomplices. If this was forthcoming the Capt guaranteed him a free pass to Australia. The prisoner then disclosed to the Capt how he had seen IRA men at Clonmult and meeting a military party on his way to Cork, he informed a military officer and that he himself led the party down to their camp. For this he received a lump sum and was taken on as a permanent paid spy at £1 per week and the promise of a lump sum for any good catch made on his information. He then gave the names of those already forwarded to you as paid spies.
4. David Walsh was subsequently tried by court-martial for espionage and found guilty and sentenced to be shot. The finding was confirmed by our Bn O/C and the sentence was duly executed.

Signed Adjutant, Glenville Company.

David Walsh's remains were subsequently secretly buried in the old cemetery of Doonpeter, Glenville, Co. Cork.

The IRA concluded that David Walsh had been trapping rabbits near Clonmult and had spotted some of the volunteers returning from confessions in Dungourney on the Saturday evening prior to the battle. He was making his way to Cork on the Sunday morning when he stopped the British Army patrol. He then guided them to Clonmult. We now know, however, that in fact the informer brought the information to Victoria Barracks on the Sunday morning.

---

25   Glenville was designated as 'C' Company, 1st Battalion, 2nd Brigade, IRA.

The Intelligence Officer (IO) of the Fermoy Battalion of the IRA, James Coss, claimed to have located the information that led to the hunt for Walsh. He stated that:

> Amongst the information received by me, from intelligence officers in the military barracks, was a copy of a file, which gave particulars of the individual who gave the information to the enemy forces, which led to the massacre of a number of IRA men. They were I think, Midleton Battalion Column at Clonmult, in February 1921. Within twenty-four hours of receiving the information, the spy in question had been arrested, tried and executed. His name was David Walsh.[26]

Evidence gathered from the British sources suggests that Walsh, aged possibly 26 at the time, did not inform on the column at Clonmult and having been given an impossible choice admitted to doing so under extreme duress. Years later, in correspondence with the Walsh family, Gen Strickland stated that Walsh was not known to him.

The British account of the killing of Walsh is as follows:[27]

> Some idea of the method of extracting information by threats of violence is demonstrated in the case of a man named David Walsh, a detailed account of whose treatment was found in a captured document. He was arrested by the IRA, for being 'a suspicious person of the tramp class' and he was detained for two days, during which time no information could be obtained from him. In order to remedy this, he was removed to a lonely mountain, and was confronted with the parish priest and an empty grave, and informed that he was to be shot forthwith, unless he supplied them with full information concerning himself and his accomplices. If this was forthcoming, the Captain guaranteed him a free pass to Australia. The unfortunate man, with the prospect of imminent death staring him in the face, invented a bogus story as to his having met a military party on the way to Cork, and having given them information concerning a camp at Clonmult. The way in which the IRA captain fulfilled his guarantee is told in the final paragraph of the document, which reads, 'David Walsh was subsequently tried by court-martial for espio-

---

26   James Coss, *WS No. 1065*, p. 11.
27   Peter Hart, *British Intelligence in Ireland 1920–21, The Final Reports, 'Irish Narratives'*, p. 91.

nage, found guilty and sentenced to be shot. The finding was duly confirmed and the sentence duly executed.'[28]

On the morning of 28th May 1921, Comdt Diarmuid O'Hurley set off alone and on foot, armed with a revolver and a grenade, from Jack Ring's house at Ballyriorta, on the north-east side of Midleton.[29] The Cameron Highlanders were constantly raiding Carrigtwohill from their base in Cobh and the local volunteers were doing nothing about it. Comdt O'Hurley was going to meet Carrigtwohill IRA officers to admonish them for their lack of activity on the matter. He travelled around the north side of Midleton using byroads.

He was crossing the road beside the old graveyard at Gurtacrue when he was surprised by a joint RIC/British Army bicycle patrol under the command of District Inspector GHA Aylmore, RIC. Some accounts believe that RIC sergeant Joseph Coleman was in charge of the patrol. This is not possible because he had been shot dead in Midleton two weeks earlier. Comdt Hurley attempted to run from the scene but he was shot down, the 29-year-old column commander being mortally wounded.[30] Local man Patrick Keeffe witnessed the shooting while he was working in a nearby field. He could not go to the scene until the Crown Forces had departed about thirty minutes later. He knelt down beside the casualty and initially believed that it was Jack O'Connell. He found O'Hurley lying flat on his back and still breathing but in a very bad condition. The bullet had penetrated his back between the lungs, cut through his body and exited above the navel. He ran to Carrig House, where he met Batt McCarthy, whom he requested to go to Midleton to get a priest to attend to O'Hurley. When Keeffe returned to O'Hurley he found him dead. He was soon joined by local men Con Dorgan and brothers Patrick and Michael Buckley. They searched the body and found a packet containing eleven revolver bullets but no revolver, a prayer book and some personal belongings. His body was taken to Kelly's house in Carrigogna where Fr Flannery, C.C. Midleton, administered the last rights and a local lady, Ms Lena Clohessy of the Mill Cottage, recited the rosary in Irish.[31]

The British did not learn until the following day who they had killed. By then Comdt O'Hurley's body had been taken to Paddy Daly's house at

---

28   Peter Hart, *British Intelligence in Ireland 1920–21, The Final Reports*, p. 91.
29   Jack O'Connell, *WS No. 1444*, pp. 18–19.
30   UKNA, Kew, London, Military Court of Inquiry in Lieu of an Inquest on Jeremiah O'Hurley, WO 35/152/82.
31   Cork Historical and Archaeological Society, *The Gravestone Inscriptions of Co. Cork, - X, Dangandonovan Burial Ground*, by R. Henchion, p. 50.

Gurteen, just across the fields from the site of the Battle of Clonmult.[32] From there, his body was taken to Ballintotis Church, east of Midleton, and on the following day he was buried temporarily in a lead-lined coffin in Churchtown North Cemetery. At 6 am the following morning the military, having discovered the identity of the previous day's victim, arrived at Kelly's house to interrogate the household without success. On 14th September 1921, during the Truce, Diarmuid O'Hurley was re-interred in a grave adjacent to the Republican plot in Holy Rosary Cemetery, Midleton, beside some of his comrades killed at Clonmult.[33]

Three days later, on 31st May, the IRA detonated the bomb primed by Paddy Whelan at Clonmult beside the band of the Hampshire Regiment. Two Youghal volunteers, Paddy O'Reilly and Thomas Power, detonated the device, Paddy was the trigger man.[34] The band, playing 'The Viscount Nelson', was leading a company from the regiment from the army barracks in Youghal towards the shooting range west of the town, for Lewis gun practice. 'When the clouds of dust settled, some twenty men and boys were seen lying on the ground and pitiful groans and cries for help were heard. Seven members of the band were killed or died of their wounds. Corporal C. Whichelow, L/Cpl R. McCall, Bdm F. Burke, Bdm F. Washington and three Band Boys, F. Evans, G. Simmons and F. Hesterman, were killed and nineteen of the band wounded'.[35] Band Boy Hesterman, aged 14, was the youngest member of the Crown Forces to be killed during the War of Independence. No band of the Royal Hampshire Regiment played 'The Viscount Nelson' ever again.[36]

The Truce was declared at noon on Monday, 11th July 1921, the same day the mother of the two Clonmult 'boys' Michael and David Desmond passed to her eternal reward.

There was a further loss for the Hampshire Regiment before they left Ireland. In Macroom, on 26th April 1922, Lt G.R.A. Dove, who had been present at Clonmult on the day of the battle, was travelling to Killarney, along with two other officers from other regiments, Lt R.A. Hendy and Lt K.R. Henderson M.C., along with their driver Pte J.R. Brooks.[37] On their way to Killarney, they

---

32   *Rebel Cork's Fighting Story*, p.197.
33   R. Henchion, *Journal of the Cork Historical and Archaeological Society*, Vol. LXXVIII, No. 227, Jan.–Jun. 1973, pp. 49–51.
34   Patrick Whelan, *WS No. 1449*, p. 56.
35   *Regimental History of the Royal Hampshire Regiment*, Vol. 3, p. 11.
36   Lt Col Colin Bulleid, curator, Royal Hampshire Regiment Museum, Winchester, England.
37   Barry Keane, *Cork's Revolutionary Dead 1916–1923*, pp. 285–286.

stopped for some refreshments in Dick William's Hotel, Macroom. The local IRA quickly became aware of their presence. Finding all four in civilian attire and carrying concealed weapons, the IRA officers believed they were on some type of intelligence mission. It is now known that they were being followed by a local IRA officer, Frank Busteed, and some of his colleagues. Even though the Treaty had been signed and ratified and the War of Independence was over, Busteed was determined to avenge the killing of his mother by two British Army intelligence officers in March 1921. He believed that two officers in the party, including Lt Dove, were responsible.[38] All four were shot dead that night and their bodies were found at Kilgobnait, west of Macroom, approximately eighteen months later.[39]

---

38   Sean O'Callaghan, *Execution*, pp. 181–182, also pp. 189–192.
39   Patrick J. Twohig, *Green Tears for Hecuba*, pp. 337–344, also, *Cork's Revolutionary Dead 1916–1923*, pp. 286–287.

THE TRIAL BY MILITARY COURT OF CAPT PADDY HIGGINS

Captain Paddy Higgins was the eighth and last of the Clonmult prisoners to be tried by Military Court. He had been shot in the mouth following the surrender and after recovering from the wound he was found to be suffering from appendicitis. He was eventually declared fit and released from the Military Hospital on 28th April.[1] His Military Court proceedings began on Friday, 17th June 1921, when he was served with his charge sheet in his cell in the Military Detention Barracks in Cork.[2]

Paddy Higgins was charged with committing an offence: 'In that he, at Clonmult, County Cork, on the 20th of February 1921, with Jeremiah O'Leary and other persons, did levy war against his Majesty the King, by attacking a detachment of his Majesty's troops.'[3]

His trial by Military Court opened in Victoria Barracks, Cork, on Tuesday, 21st June 1921. The court consisted of three military officers acting as jurors with a fourth acting in the capacity of Judge Advocate.[4] He was defended by Mr George Daly, B.L., instructed by Mr William J. Barry, solicitor, Midleton.[5] It was noticed by the defence legal team that one of the British officers adjudicating had been involved in the first Clonmult trial. After some legal argument, this officer was replaced. When the trial recommenced, the accused pleaded not guilty.

The case for the prosecution followed on the very same lines as with his comrades. Evidence was taken from two of the British Army officers who were

1   Patrick Higgins, *WS No. 1467*, p. 4.
2   *Cork Examiner*, 28th June 1921 also Patrick Higgins, *WS No. 1467*.
3   *Cork Examiner*, 22nd June 1921.
4   *Ibid*. 28th June 1921.
5   *Ibid*. 22nd June 1921.

at Clonmult and from an unnamed soldier who was sent for reinforcements, petrol and bombs. The court also heard from two members of the RIC present at Clonmult and the night ward master, a RAMC corporal on duty at the Central Military Hospital at Victoria Barracks when the wounded Higgins was brought in for treatment. Evidence was given identifying Higgins as being present and of being captured after the battle, and it was also stated that he had not attempted to escape.[6]

The accused was examined on the first day of the trial. He stated that he was 23 years old and resided with his parents at Ardra, Rostellan, Co. Cork. His defence rested upon the claim that he could not have been a member of the IRA due to his delicate physical condition. This stemmed from eight year's earlier when, as a pupil at St Colman's College, Fermoy, he was diagnosed with appendicitis. The operation was not fully successful and he had an ongoing problem with his appendix.

As with his comrades during the first Clonmult trial, Higgins gave a totally false account of his activities in the weeks leading to the battle and during the battle. He stated that, during November 1920, the military had raided his home and this had frightened his mother to such an extent that she had pleaded with him to go on the run. He moved to a motor firm in Clonmel, County Tipperary, but he had returned home on 14th February when his appendix became inflamed again. He moved to a relative's house near Conna, on Saturday, 19th February, the day before the battle. He further stated that he went to Midleton with his uncle, where he met a school friend, Dick Hegarty, who took him to the farmhouse in Clonmult and there he spent the night. He claimed not to have known any of the men he met in the farmhouse. He went to 8.30 am mass the following day. He had his Sunday dinner in his sister's house and stated that the only reason he went back to the farmhouse was to retrieve some item he had left there. He was in the farmyard, pumping the tyre of his bicycle, when the British troops arrived and that is how he came to be trapped in the house. He stated he had not seen arms in the house and had not taken any part in the attack.[7]

Cross-examined by the prosecutor, the defendant stated that he was not a member of the IRA. He had been a member of the old Volunteers but had resigned as he was too delicate.[8]

---

6   *Cork Examiner* and Appendix 'A' to Patrick Higgins WS.
7   *Cork Examiner*, 22nd June 1921.
8   *Ibid.*

His mother was next called to give evidence. She stated that following the military raid on 16th November, she had advised her son to move in with his uncle. His uncle was next called and he confirmed that he had taken the accused to Midleton on the day before the battle and had seen him leave with a friend. A sister of the accused gave evidence of seeing her brother at mass with a friend on the morning of the battle. She also stated that Higgins had dinner in her house after mass and had returned to the farmhouse only because he had left something behind. The second and last day of the trial was taken up with the summary of evidence. Following this the Judge Advocate reviewed the evidence and the court was closed.

Following the end of the trial on 22nd June, Higgins was informed two nights later while in his cell that he had been found guilty of the charges against him.[9] He was sentenced to death, the court had made no recommendation for mercy, and the sentence was subject to confirmation. The following day his legal team immediately lodged an appeal with the Chancery Division in Dublin.

His appeal was heard in Dublin on Wednesday, 27th June, before the Master of the Rolls, Sir Charles O'Connor. Mr Hugh Kennedy, K.C., Mr Patrick Lynch, K.C., and Mr John A. Costello (later Taoiseach), instructed by Mr William Barry, appeared on behalf of the plaintiff.

A writ was issued on his behalf claiming that the Military Court did not have the authority to try him, that military tribunals could only be set up by an Act of Parliament, that he was not subject to military law, and that a state of war did not exist in the Martial Law area. The plaintiff also sought an interlocutory injunction, pending the hearing of his claim, for the declaration of the right to enable him to have the question of constitutional right finally decided by the ultimate tribunal if necessary. This ultimate authority was the House of Lords. The plaintiff also sought relief by injunction, writ of habeas corpus or otherwise so as to prevent the defendants or any of them or any officer of the military or civil executive from imperilling the life and interfering with the liberty of the plaintiff.[10]

Following this, the appeal court heard the evidence that was presented at his trial. The point was made that there was grave reason to fear that the plaintiff was in imminent peril of his life, in that the sentence of death might be carried out at any moment and without any further notice unless the court intervened to prevent it. The Master of the Rolls granted a conditional order for a writ of

---

9   Patrick Higgins, *WS No. 1467*, p. 7.
10   *Cork Examiner*, 28th June 1921.

habeas corpus directed to Gen Macready, Gen Strickland, and the Governor of the Detention Barracks, Cork.[11] This writ put a temporary stay on his execution.

Before the findings of his first appeal were announced, his legal team made a fresh appeal on Tuesday, 19th July. This appeal was heard, again by the Master of the Rolls, in the Chancery Division in Dublin. This appeal was for an order making absolute the conditional order for a writ of habeas corpus made by the Master of the Rolls on 27th June.[12]

An issue that was raised during this appeal was why the prisoner was not tried before a formal Field General Court Martial as against a Military Court. The Crown's lawyers were unable to answer this point. The Master of the Rolls reserved judgement and directed that a telegram should be sent to the military, arresting the sentence passed on the plaintiff.[13]

This appeal was overshadowed by another appeal that was ongoing, before the House of Lords in London, involving two Cork men under sentence of death who had been captured in possession of firearms and ammunition. Patrick Clifford and Michael O'Sullivan were arrested in April and following their trial were sentenced to death. The Irish Court of Appeal dismissed a subsequent appeal, holding that it was a criminal cause or matter, and that therefore, no appeal lay.[14] The case was then brought to the House of Lords, where it opened on Thursday, 7th July. The hearing was adjourned on Tuesday, 12th July, the day after the Truce came into effect. The following Thursday it was announced that judgement was reserved in the appeal.[15] Events had overtaken circumstances, the guns had fallen silent since noon on Monday, 11th July, the War of Independence was over and there could be no further executions as long as the Truce held. Nevertheless, the legal appeals continued and Paddy Higgins' case was tied in with the appeal of a Clare prisoner, John Joseph Egan, convicted of possession of ammunition and sentenced to death. Their appeals lead to a major legal battle between the British Army and the civil courts. The disputed events and Military Courts were taking place in the Martial Law Area, but Dublin, seat of the High Court, was not under Martial Law.[16] The Army could not publicly acknowledge the supremacy of the civil court without undermining the Military Courts.

---

11   *Cork Examiner*, 28th June 1921.
12   *Ibid.* 20th July 1921.
13   *Ibid.*
14   *Ibid.* 8th July 1921.
15   *Cork Examiner*, 15th July 1921.
16   *The Trial of Civilians by Military Courts Ireland 1921*, p. 110.

After two days of legal arguments, the Master of the Rolls gave his judgement. He severely criticised the exercise of their powers by the Military Authorities and

> contrasted the fairness of the Court Martial procedure with that of Military Courts, which in these instances had, in his reading, exceeded the bounds of the Act. Held that a state of war being in existence at the date of the passing of the Restoration of Order in Ireland Act 1920, the executive powers of the Military Authority were limited by the Act and that accordingly an offence punishable by death should be tried by Court-Martial. Every subject of the King was at least entitled to be legally tried and legally convicted. Both prisoners were tried by Military Court not by a Court-Martial, but in a Court constituted in some way not known to the law, by some Military Officers.

The Master of the Rolls ruled that the writs of habeas corpus would issue and that the Crown must produce the prisoners in court on Friday the 29th. Gen Macready telegraphed Dublin GHQ with orders to ignore the writs. Having failed to produce the prisoners in court on the date set, the Master of the Rolls issued a writ of attachment, in effect writs for the arrest of Gen Macready, Strickland and Brig-Gen Cameron.

The impasse between Gen Macready and the Master of the Rolls was only cleared the next day when the government in Westminster gave way and ordered the release of both Egan and Higgins.[17] Both men were immediately released.

The five other surviving prisoners captured at the Battle of Clonmult remained in military custody throughout the remainder of 1921. Very shortly after the executions of their comrades, the five men – Jeremiah O'Leary, John Harty, William Garde, Edmond Terry and Robert Walsh – were transferred from the Military Detention Barracks to Cork Male Gaol, off Western Road in Cork City. From there on 30th April, all five were part of a larger group transferred to the 'Military Prison in the Field' on Spike Island, which was for convicted Republican prisoners and internees.[18] By coincidence, Spike Island was opened as a military prison and as an internment camp on 19th February 1921, the day before the Battle of Clonmult.[19] On 17th November 1921, all five were part of a large group of prisoners transferred from Spike Island to the civilian prison

---

17   *Ibid.* p. 113.
18   Spike Island Republican prisoners and internees data bases.
19   *Cork Examiner*, 21 February 1921.

in Kilkenny.[20] Later they were transferred to Waterford Prison, from where they were released in February 1922.[21]

The Anglo–Irish Treaty was signed in 10 Downing Street, London, on 6th December 1921 and all internees were immediately released. This Treaty was ratified by Dáil Éireann, at Westminster and in Northern Ireland one month later, on 7th January. The War of Independence was over. All the convicted Republican prisoners were released from custody during the following days.

---

20   Spike Island Republican prisoners and internees databases.
21   D. O'Leary, *WS No. 1589*, p. 12.

THE BATTLE OF
CLONMULT CONCLUSION

For the Crown Forces, the outcome of the Battle of Clonmult was a morale booster. It had combined the use of good intelligence, the timely deployment of their forces to Clonmult, and the effective tactics employed throughout the battle. It was one of the few occasions during the War of Independence that the Crown Forces wiped out a flying column.

I have concluded that the legal battles fought by the IRA's legal representatives both during the Military Courts trials and the subsequent appeals must be judged as a partial success. The eight men captured were liable to suffer death, but the fact that just two were executed was testament to the hard work of their legal teams. The legal battle, especially the appeals in Dublin, also had the effect of neutralising, to some extent, the powers of the military governors in the Martial Law area. The death penalties handed down by Military Courts would have to be confirmed by the senior civil courts in Dublin and London.

For the IRA, the outcome of the battle was confirmation that the policy and tactics of a guerrilla-style campaign was the only way of doing battle with the Crown Forces. Conventional warfare had to be avoided at all costs. This included a guerrilla-style action developing into a conventional one.

For the IRA leadership at battalion and company level, Clonmult must have brought home to them their lack of formal military training and experience. This lack of experience was apparent not only prior to the battle, but at all stages during it. The outcome of the battle highlighted this deficiency. The fact that the commander had stayed at Clonmult so long, the composition of the Reconnaissance Group, the fact that the sentries were prepared to leave their posts, and that the officer in command at the time allowed this, highlighted a lack of leadership, particularly in the heat of battle. There was no shortage of volunteers and of bravery, but there was a lack of experienced and effective leadership.

The high numbers of men who volunteered for active service with the flying columns across the country is testament to their bravery. These men were willing to participate in engagements against a vastly superior force. The Crown Forces were superior in numbers, weapons, experience, training; indeed superior in all aspects on war fighting. By volunteering for active service the Volunteers were also showing that they were prepared to sacrifice their lives for the freedom of their country.

An astonishing statistic is that of the twenty members of the 4th Battalion Flying Column present at Clonmult on 20th February 1921, fifteen of them, or 75 per cent, had lost their lives by the Truce on 11th July.

It was at local level that the effects of the Battle of Clonmult were felt most. The battle was a devastating blow to the fighting efficiency of the 4th Battalion in Cork. The battalion's flying column, effectively wiped out at Clonmult, had been its fighting echelon. The men who were killed and those that were captured had been the backbone of the column. There were others who were prepared to take their place, but the weapons and ammunition so successfully captured during the skirmishes of 1920 could not be replaced. The RIC barracks were now too well guarded and the British Army patrols were too strong and constantly on the alert.

For many years afterwards, Clonmult was the one battle most often spoken of by the surviving Cork veterans of the War of Independence. This was primarily because of the number of their comrades killed there; after all, it was the IRA's greatest loss in a single battle. In time, however, the victories at Kilmichael, Crossbarry and other locations took the limelight. It was sweeter to speak of battles won than of a battle lost.

LIST OF APPENDICES

APPENDIX 1

WEEKEND CASUALTIES, 19TH–20TH FEBRUARY 1921

Midleton...13	
Skibbereen..2	
Galway Councillor................................1	
Limerick Boys.....................................2	
Ex-Soldier in Cork..............................1	
Tipperary Labourer.............................1	
Armagh Farmer...................................1	
Train Mystery.....................................1	
Clones Tragedy....................................1	
Body found in River.............................1	
Total	24

[1]

---

[1] *Freeman's Journal*, Monday, 21st February 1921.

APPENDIX 2

THE IRA ORDER OF BATTLE 1921 PERTAINING TO CLONMULT

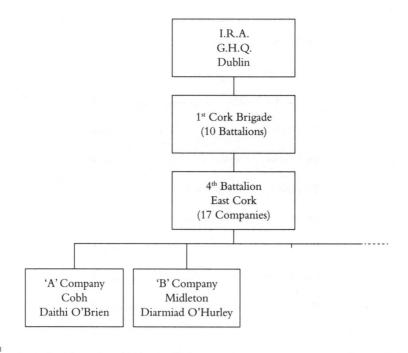

I.R.A.
G.H.Q.
Dublin

1ˢᵗ Cork Brigade
(10 Battalions)

4ᵗʰ Battalion
East Cork
(17 Companies)

'A' Company
Cobh
Daithi O'Brien

'B' Company
Midleton
Diarmiad O'Hurley

[1]

The members of the flying column killed at Clonmult were drawn primarily from 'A' and 'B' Companies, 4th Battalion, 1st Cork Brigade. Comdt Michael Leahy of Cobh was the Commanding Officer of the Battalion at the time.[2]

1   *Capuchin Annual*, 1970, p. 360.
2   *Ibid*.

APPENDIX 3

4TH BATTALION FLYING COLUMN, MEMBERS PRESENT AT CLONMULT

Comdt Diarmuid O'Hurley	Bandon	killed 28th May 1921
Vice-Comdt Joseph Ahern	Midleton	
Capt James Ahern	Cobh	killed 20th February 1921
Capt Richard Hegarty	Garryvoe	killed 20th February 1921
Capt Paddy Higgins	Cloyne	
Capt Jack O'Connell	Cobh	
Capt Diarmuid O'Leary	Killeagh	
Capt Paddy Whelan	Wexford and Cobh	
Lt Christopher O'Sullivan	Midleton	killed 20th February 1921
Lt Patrick O'Sullivan	Cobh	executed 28th April 1921
Vol Jeremiah Ahern	Midleton	killed 20th February 1921
Vol Liam Ahern	Midleton	killed 20th February 1921
Vol Donal Dennehy	Midleton	killed 20th February 1921
Vol David Desmond	Midleton	killed 20th February 1921
Vol Michael Desmond	Midleton	killed 20th February 1921
Vol James Glavin	Cobh	killed 20th February 1921
Vol Michael Hallahan	Midleton	killed 20th February 1921
Vol John Joe Joyce	Midleton	killed 20th February 1921
Vol Maurice Moore	Cobh	executed 28th April 1921
Vol Joseph Morrissey	Castlemartyr & Carlow	killed 20th February 1921
Na Fianna Vol John Harty	Cloyne	
Na Fianna Vol Edmond Terry	Churchtown South	
William Garde	Shanagarry	
Robert Walsh	Ballycotton	

APPENDIX 4

NOMINAL ROLL OF THE 4TH BATTALION FLYING COLUMN

Comdt Diarmuid O'Hurley	Officer Commanding	Bandon
Vice-Comdt Joseph Ahern	Second-in-Command	Midleton
Capt Paddy Higgins	Quartermaster Officer	Cloyne
Capt James Ahern		Cobh
Capt Richard Hegarty		Garryvoe
Capt Jack O'Connell		Cobh
Capt Diarmuid O'Leary		Killeagh
Capt Paddy Whelan		Wexford and Cobh
Lt John Kelleher		Midleton
Lt Christopher O'Sullivan		Midleton
Lt Patrick O'Sullivan		Cobh
Vol Jack Ahern		Midleton
Vol Jeremiah Ahern		Midleton
Vol Liam Ahern		Midleton
Vol Tom Buckley		Midleton
Vol James Cagney		Midleton
Vol Daniel Cashman		Midleton
Vol Richard Crowley		Midleton.
Vol Donal Dennehy		Midleton
Vol David Desmond		Midleton
Vol Michael Desmond		Midleton
Vol Joseph Duhig		Midleton
Vol James Glavin		Cobh
Vol James Glavin		Cobh
Vol Michael Hallahan		Midleton
Vol Jack Hyde		Ballinacurra
Vol Philip Hyde		Midleton
Vol Tom Hyde		Ballinacurra
Vol John Joe Joyce		Midleton

Vol Michael Kearney	Midleton
Vol Maurice Moore	Cobh
Vol Joseph Morrissey	Castlemartyr & Carlow
Vol Michael Murnane	Midleton
Vol Jim McCarthy	Midleton
Vol David Stanton	Midleton
Vol Patrick White	?

Note

There were normally just three appointments in a flying column for officers. The other officers listed were officers in their local Volunteer companies and operating in the column as Volunteers.

APPENDIX 5

THE BATTLE OF CLONMULT TIMELINE

Sep 1920 4th Battalion Flying Column formed at Knockraha.

11 Dec Flying column surrounded in a house in Cloyne by British soldiers.

29 Dec Column attacked an RIC foot patrol in Midleton, three constables killed.

Dec 1920–Jan 1921 The column was based in Kilmountain, Midleton, and later in Cottstown, Dungourney.

6 Jan Column relocated to disused farmhouse at Garrylaurence, Clonmult.

17 Feb The column received a mission from Brigade HQ to attack a train carrying troops and military stores from Queenstown (Cobh) to Cork. Cobh Junction was selected as the ambush position.

19 Feb Members of the column walked to Dungourney for their confessions and were spotted by an informer on their return journey.

Sunday, 20 Feb 1921, Battle of Clonmult, approximate times

12 pm The column commander, Comdt D. O'Hurley, Vice-Comdt J. Ahern and Capt P. Whelan departed the farmhouse by car for Cobh Junction to carry out a reconnaissance for the forthcoming attack on a train.

Capt J. O'Connell was ordered to move the column out from Clonmult after dark.

12 pm Information is received at Victoria Barracks, Cork, as to the possible location of members of a flying column near Clonmult.

12.30 pm Based on information received, a British Army mobile patrol is assembled, briefed and prepared to depart Victoria Barracks, Cork, for Clonmult, under the command of Lt D.F. Hook, M.C., 2nd Battalion, Hampshire Regiment.

12.30 pm John Harty and Edmond Terry departed Churchtown South for Clonmult. On the journey they met Robert Walsh and William Garde and all four cycled to Clonmult.

2 pm Dick Hegarty arrived in Clonmult and met the four cyclists.

2.15 pm British Army mobile patrol departed Victoria Barracks via Midleton for Clonmult.

3 pm The British Army mobile patrol arrived at Rathorgan Cross Roads, Clonmult.

3.10 pm The patrol was broken into three groups and set off to search Carey's house.

3.20 pm Army patrols surrounded and searched Carey's house believing this was the location of the members of the column. The house was empty and they decided to search another house nearby.

3.30 pm Dick Hegarty and the four cyclists arrived at the farmhouse.

3.45 pm Lt Koe's foot patrol arrived at the farmhouse. A shootout resulted in the deaths of Volunteers Michael Desmond and John Joe Joyce.

3.50 pm Lt Hook's foot patrol also arrived and during an attempted break out Jack O'Connell escaped and James Ahern, Michael Hallahan and Richard Hegarty were killed.

4.15 pm Lt Hook sent three soldiers to Midleton RIC Barracks for reinforcements.

5.20 pm Auxiliary Police and RIC reinforcements arrived at Garrylaurence.

5.50 pm Lt Hammond set fire to the thatch roof of the farmhouse.

6 pm Farmhouse was on fire and those inside were compelled to surrender.

6.10 pm Twelve members of the column surrendered and exited the farmhouse.

6.15 pm Auxiliary Police opened fire on their prisoners and seven were shot dead.

7 pm Crown Forces and eight prisoners departed the farmhouse for the vehicles.

7.30 pm Crown Forces convoy departed Rathorgan Cross Roads for Midleton.

9 pm Crown Forces convoy arrived back at Victoria Barracks, Cork.

9.30 pm The five wounded prisoners were taken to the Military Hospital and the remaining three to 'The Cage'.

24 Feb The nine men killed at Clonmult were buried in Midleton and two in Cobh.

25 Feb Dick Hegarty was buried in Ballymacoda.

8 March Trial by Military Court of the Clonmult prisoners began in Victoria Barracks, Cork. All were charged with 'Levying War against the King'.

March All seven were found guilty. Patrick O'Sullivan, Maurice Moore and Diarmuid O'Leary were sentenced to death. John Harty, Edmond Terry, William Garde and Robert Walsh were sentenced to Penal Servitude for Life.

28 April Patrick O'Sullivan and Maurice were executed in the Detention Barracks in Cork and buried in Cork Male Gaol. Diarmuid O'Leary's sentence was commuted to Penal Servitude for Life.

30 April The five convicted prisoners are transferred to Spike Island.

June The eighth prisoner, Patrick Higgins, was tried by Military Court, found guilty and sentenced to death.

11 July The Truce came into effect.

July Patrick Higgins appeal went before the Master of the Rolls in London, where eventually his appeal succeeded and he was released.

17 November The five Clonmult prisoners were transferred from Spike Island to Kilkenny Prison and later transferred to Waterford Prison.

6 December The Treaty was signed in London and all internees were released.

7 January 1922 The Treaty was ratified, the War of Independence was over and all Republican prisoners were released from custody.

APPENDIX 6

IRISH WAR OF INDEPENDENCE MEDALS

1917–21 Service Medals and the Truce Commemorative Medal 1971[1]

The medals with 'Comrac' (Warrior) bar, below left, were awarded to persons who rendered active service in operations against Crown Forces between 1 April 1920 and 11th July 1921, the day the Truce began.[2] The medals without bar, below centre, were awarded to non-combatants, but who were members of the IRA, the Cumann na mBan and na Fíanna Eireann or the Irish Citizen Army for the three months ended on 11th July 1921.[3] Both medals were awarded officially named and numbered to all IRA men and women that were killed during the War of Independence as well as to those that were entitled to the medal but had died prior to its presentation in 1941. All other recipients received the medal unnamed. In 1971 all surviving recipients of both medals received the Truce Commemorative Medal, below right.

---

1   E.H. O'Toole, *Decorations and Medals of the Republic of Ireland* (Medallic Publishing Company, Connecticut, U.S.A., 1990), pp. 25–27.

2   *The Military Service (1916–1923) Pensions Collection, the Medals Series*, Defence Forces Printing Press, 2016, p. 9. Also, *Medals of the Irish Defence Forces*, (DFPP), 2010, p. 94.

3   *Ibid.*

APPENDIX 7

BRITISH ARMY ORDER OF BATTLE, 1921

The headquarters of the British Army in Ireland was located at Parkgate, Dublin, and had the title Headquarters Irish Command.[1] At the time of Clonmult it was under the command of Gen Sir Neville Macready.[2] The Irish Command was sub-divided into divisions and Munster was within the area of operations of the British Army's 6th Division under the command of Gen Sir E.P. Strickland, with his headquarters in Victoria Barracks, Cork.[3] The forces under Gen Strickland were estimated at 12,600 soldiers, Auxiliaries and Black and Tans, excluding naval personnel.[4] The 6th Division was further divided into two brigades, of which the 17th Infantry Brigade was based in Victoria Barracks, Cork, under the command of Col Cmdt H.W. Higginson, C.B., D.S.O. Col Cmdt Higginson was also the Military Governor of the area that included East Cork.[5]

The 2nd Battalion, Hampshire Regiment, was one of the four infantry battalions of the 17th Infantry Brigade.[6] The British troops that were the first to arrive at Clonmult were drawn from this battalion. It was also stationed in Victoria Barracks and was under the command of Col C.N. French.[7] The British Army mobile patrol to Clonmult was under the command of Lt D.F. Hook, M.C., 2nd Battalion, Hampshire Regiment.

1   *Rebel Corks Fighting Story*, p. 206.
2   *Rebel Corks Fighting Story*, p. 70.
3   *Rebel Corks Fighting Story*, p. 206.
4   *Ibid.*
5   Notice 'B' Notice for destruction of property, Appendix 12.
6   Charles Townshend, *The British Campaign in Ireland 1919–1921*, pp. 53 and 144.
7   *Regimental History of the Royal Hampshire Regiment*, Vol. 3, p. 9.

BRITISH ARMY ORDER OF BATTLE PERTAINING TO CLONMULT[1]

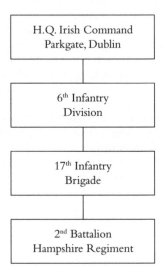

The British Army personnel involved in the Battle of Clonmult were drawn from the 2nd Battalion, Hampshire Regiment, Victoria Barracks, Cork City.

---

1   Townshend, *The British Campaign in Ireland 1919–1921*, pp. 53 and 144.

APPENDIX 9

CROWN FORCES PERSONNEL KNOWN TO HAVE BEEN AT CLONMULT[1]

2nd Battalion, The Hampshire Regiment

Lt D.F. Hook, M.C., patrol commander
Lt G.R.A. Dove
Lt A.R. Koe

31275, CSM Edward Corney, MM

5486043, Sgt S.E.T. Mantle
5485280, Cpl G. Carter
5486719, Pte A. Murhall
5486558, Pte C. Sherry
5486823, Pte C. Vautier

The Dorsetshire Regiment and Intelligence Dept., Cork
Lt H. Hammond, M.C.

Royal Irish Constabulary (Black and Tans)
Constable Henry Harris
Constable A.B.D. Smith

---

1   Names extracted from Military Court documents and lists of awards. Full list not found, author.

APPENDIX 10

BRITISH MILITARY COMMUNIQUÉS, 20TH AND 22ND FEBRUARY 1921

Communiqué Issued by Military General Headquarters on the Night of Sunday, 20th February

This afternoon a party of the 2nd Battalion Hampshire Regiment surprised a party of armed civilians in a house near Midleton, Co. Cork (Martial Law area). The civilians split up, some taking up positions in the garden of the house, others firing from the house itself. After a fight of nearly two hours' duration three wounded and five unwounded men were captured and thirteen were found dead.

A number of service rifles and a quantity of ammunition and bombs were also seized by the troops. One soldier was slightly wounded.[1]

Tuesday, 22nd February

An official communiqué issued by General Headquarters, Parkgate, states:

> Further official details of the conflict which took place near Midleton, Co. Cork on Sunday, shows that a desperate defence was put up by the rebels who were eventually compelled to leave the open and take cover in the house.
>
> Police reinforcements were quickly on the scene and the house was set on fire to drive out the defenders. Some came running out of the house, with their hands up, while others continued to fire on the Crown Forces as they went to accept the surrender.
>
> The Commandant of the Midleton Company Irish Republican Army was amongst those killed. In addition to a large quantity of bombs, rifles and ammunition, a motor car was also captured.[2]

---

1   *Freeman's Journal*, Monday, 21st February 1921.
2   *Ibid*.

APPENDIX 11

NOTICE 'B' DESTRUCTION OF PROPERTY BY CROWN FORCES

WHEREAS ON the 17th day of May, 1921, cowardly and murderous attacks were carried out by armed rebels against the Forces of the Crown in the MIDLETON district,
and whereas there are good grounds for believing that you are a supporter of such rebels,
Now, therefore, I, COLONEL COMMANDANT, H.W. HIGGINSON, C.B., D.S.O. Commanding 17th Infantry Brigade and Military Governor, have ordered the destruction of your home.
Given under my hand at Cork this 17th day of May, 1921.

H.W. HIGGINSON
Colonel-Commandant
Military Governor

To:-

THOMAS CASHMAN,
BALLINROSTIG.[1]

---

1   Cashman family artefacts.

APPENDIX 12

LT A.R. KOE'S BATTLE OF CLONMULT REPORT

Report of operations carried out by a party of the 2nd Battalion, Hampshire Regiment, and a party of Auxiliary Police, on 20th February 1921.[1]

Reference attached Map and Ordnance Survey Map: 1in to 1 Mile. Sheet 187 and 188.

(1)   A party of Second Battalion Hampshire Regiment consisting of 4 Officers, 21 other ranks and two RASC drivers left Victoria Barracks at 14.15 hours on the 20. 2. 1921.

(2)   This party arrived at Cross Roads, 300 yards due south of 'T' in RATHORGAN, about 5 miles North of MIDLETON, at 15.00 hours.

(3)   Leaving 1 N.C.O., 6 O.R.'s and the 2 drivers in charge of the lorries, the remainder of the party proceeded across to a cottage (not shown on map sheet 187 and 188); 400 yards North of the 'T' in RATHORGAN.

(4)   This cottage was searched without result. It was then decided to search a house, 400 yards N.E. of this cottage. This house is shown on map (sheet 187) and is east of GARRYLAURENCE WOOD.

(5)   The party moved there in two bodies. One consisting of Lt's HAMMOND, M.C. and KOE, CSM Corney and 7 O.R.'s and the other of Lt's HOOK, M.C. and DOVE and 6 O.R.s.

(6)   Lt KOE and his party arrived near the house while the other party were 500 yards to the west of it. They arrived at approximately 15.45 hours.

(7)   Fire was immediately opened on the leading party when they came near the house. This party was approximately in the position shown in position 1 on attached sketch. *(Not found.)*

---

1   UKNA, Kew, London, WO 35/88B.

(8)   Lt Koe and one man took cover in the lane EAST of the house. Four men from this party were lining the fence the WEST of the house.

(9)   Lt Hook M.C. and his party arrived at the fence west of the house at approximately 15.50 hours, and killed four men who were trying to escape.

(10)   Lt Koe and one man joined Lt Hook M.C. at 16.05 hours.

(11)   Three men were sent back to the lorries, which were ordered back to MIDLETON for bombs and reinforcements.

(12)   Firing continued on both sides without result and it was feared that the result might be a stalemate owing to the inferior numbers of Crown Forces, but, reinforcements began to arrive under the County Inspector, Cork (South) who, himself, came on the scene at 17.20 hours. (Total reinforcements, 1 officer and 24 O.R.'s. (Auxiliary Police)).

(13)   Lt Hammond, M.C. at 17.50 hours climbed over the fence north of the house (at a point marked (.) in the attached sketch, (*not found*), and set alight to the thatched roof of the house and directly afterwards bombs were thrown through the breach in the roof made by the fire.
        The RIC suffered one casualty (severely wounded) during this period.

(14)   At 18.20 hours the rebels signified that they wished to surrender and they were ordered to put up their hands and come out one by one. At 18.30 hours, six or seven rebels came out with their hands up and the Crown Forces went to meet them. On this fire was again opened by the remaining rebels in the house.

(15)   Fire was at once re-opened on the house by the | Crown Forces, and, in the cross fire which resulted, it was inevitable that casualties should be inflicted on the rebels outside the house by both sides.
        The Crown Forces, having re-opened fire, rushed the house. When the house was captured, there were eight men in it, four wounded and four un-wounded. These were taken prisoners.

(16)   CSM CORNEY who was with Lt Koe was wounded when the rebels first opened fire. He was sent back to the lorries and while he was on his way to them, he was threatened with a bomb by a man who had escaped from the house during the first 5 minutes and who had already attempted to shoot Lt Hammond but has missed him at point blank range. CSM Corney got away from this man, who was shot by one of the party guarding the lorries when he was actually trying to throw the bomb.
        This man by his description is believed to be the man 'JER. HURLEY', the captain of the MIDLETON Active Service COY., IRA and is known to have been the leader of all IRA activity in this area for some months.

(17)   All arms and ammunition etc. were collected, but the numbers have not yet been ascertained definitely. They amount to about 10 – 15 rifles, some shot guns, and between 6 and 10 revolvers and automatics.

(18) Appendix 'A' shows list of killed, as far as can be ascertained. (*Not found.*)

(19) Appendix 'B' shows list of wounded and un-wounded prisoners. (*Not found.*)

(20) The Crown Forces returned to Barracks arriving back at 21.00 hours.

    (Sgd) A.R. KOE, Lt   2nd Bn The Hampshire Regiment.
                                  Cork, 20.2.21.

APPENDIX 13

COL FRENCH'S LETTER OF COMMENDATION[1]

<u>**SECRET**</u>

Headquarters, 17th Infantry Brigade,

I forward herewith Lt Koe's report on operations carried out near Clonmult on 20.2.21. I allowed these operations to be carried out by the troops in the Cork area in order to save time and because the information on which they were based was obtained in Cork.

I consider that the operation was well conceived and troops skilfully led and that the whole affair reflects the highest credit on both officers and men engaged.

I have much pleasure in bringing to your notice the names of Lt A.R. Koe and Lt Hammond M.C. The former of these officers was responsible for initiating and planning the operation and I should be glad if his name might be forwarded for a suitable decoration, and if possible the Military Cross. Apart from this affair he has done consistently good work.

Lt Hammond's action in setting light to the thatched roof of the house was an exceeding gallant one which was largely responsible for the final result being achieved with so few casualties. I hope his name may be forwarded for suitable decoration. If possible a bar to his Military Cross.

I have already forwarded Lt Hook's name for a decoration in connection with another affair and merely draw your attention to the fact that he was present on this occasion also and led his party skilfully.

In conclusion I consider it essential that on such occasions Officers would always carry rifles and that there should be a Very flare pistol with every lorry load of troops as a Very Light would probably set light to a thatched roof and in any case would be an unpleasant projectile to fire into a house. Stick Rifle Grenades would also be most useful in this sort of fighting.

---

1   UKNA, Kew, London, WO 35/88B.

I trust that the D.C. Cork may be informed that the support of the RIC was timely, loyal and decisive and their ready and skilful co-operation was greatly appreciated both by the Officers and Troops concerned and also all ranks of this battalion.

(Sgd) C. French, Colonel, Officer Commanding,
       2nd Battalion, Hampshire Regiment,
       Cork, 21.2.21.

APPENDIX 14

RIC MONTHLY CONFIDENTIAL REPORT, FEBRUARY 1921

SECRET
Crime Special

County Inspector's Office
Cork. 3-3-1921.

I beg to report that the state of the City and Riding is most unsatisfactory. Murders and attempts to murder are considerably on the increase, and many reports of ambushes in preparation for Crown Forces have been received. These outrages are attributable to the work of the Sinn Féin organisation.

On Sunday 20th ult, a party of rebels in ambush were surprised by both police and military at Garrylaurence, North of Midleton, in the Youghal District. Only one of the party succeeded in getting away. From information received this man was away at a farm house for supplies, the remainder, 21 in number, were either killed, wounded, or taken prisoners. The rebels first engaged a small party of Military from a house situated in an isolated position. The house had been put in a state of defence, and on the arrival of the police they were directing a heavy fire from it. They were dislodged by firing the roof and by bombing. They then tried to escape by a ruse. Some came from the building while those that remained inside opened fire on the police and military. The whole party was at once rushed and overcome. Fortunately, the casualties to the Crown Forces were light, 1 soldier and 1 policeman being severely wounded and 1 officer and 2 police being slightly wounded. The rebels suffered 13 killed, 4 wounded, and 4 unwounded prisoners, of these 2 died subsequently. A large quantity of ammunition, as well as service rifles, shot guns and revolvers were seized. The leader of the rebel gang – Jeremiah Hurley – who had been operating in this District for a considerable time is believed to have been killed in this attack, but the body was taken away during the night. It was the only body removed.

Signed J.J.T. Carroll T.C.I.[1]

---

1   British in Ireland, Reel No. 74, Jan–March 1921, *RIC County Inspector's Monthly Confidential Report, February 1921,* CO 904/114.

BRITISH MILITARY MEDALS AWARDED FOR THE CLONMULT ACTION

The British Empire Medal (B.E.M.) awarded to Pte Clarence G. Vautier, 2nd Battalion, The Hampshire Regiment

5486823, Vautier, Clarence, G. Pte, 2nd Hampshires. The award of the British Empire Medal was announced in the *London Gazette* on 21st April 1921, (dated 1st April 1921).

The citation for the award stated: 'During an action on the 20th of February, 1921. Private Vautier held a one man snipers post, in a very exposed position for over three hours being all the time under intermittent fire at a range of from 20 to 30 yards, and succeeded in silencing the enemy fire and prevented them from forcing an entrance into the house which the Crown Forces were holding.'[1]

This incident, in which 12 IRA men were killed, occurred at Clonmult Co. Cork. The medal was presented in Dublin Castle on 12th July 1921.

Order of the British Empire (O.B.E.) awarded to Lt H. Hammond, M.C., for Clonmult[2]

Citation for the award of his O.B.E. stated: 'In the Martial Law Area, a house containing armed rebels strongly posted was surrounded by Crown Forces. A heavy fire was being directed on the troops who could make no progress. Lt Hammond M.C., under point blank fire, made his way with a tin of petrol to between two of the windows from which fire was being directed. He saturated the roof with petrol and set it alight, thus causing the death or capture of the whole rebel party.'

---

1   M.D. Cassell, 'Awards of the Medal of the Order of the British Empire for Gallantry in Ireland, 1920 to 1922', in, *The Journal of the Orders and Medals Research Society (U.K.)* Vol. No. 25, Winter 1986, No. 4, (193), p. 213.
2   UKNA, Kew, WO 35/181, medal awards at Dublin Castle, 12th July 1921. Also, www.cairogang.com.

Capt Hammond O.B.E., M.C., died of disease while serving with the Iraq Levies, 23 November 1923. He was buried in Iraq.

M.B.E. awarded to Lt A.R. Koe[3]

His citation stated: 'Lt Koe has on several occasions been responsible for the capture of rebels and large numbers of arms and exposed himself to great danger to obtain valuable information.'

M.B.E. awarded to Lt Denys Frederick Hook, M.C.[4]

The citation for the award of his M.B.E. was as follows: 'On the 28th Sept 1920 Lt Hook set out with a small party on a special lorry of his own design, constructed with a view to making it dangerous for rebels to interfere with broken down lorries. He arranged for his lorry to break down near Ballymakeera, where it was then attacked by rebels. Not wishing the identity of the lorry to be disclosed, Lt Hook allowed the rebels to come up close, some actually boarding the lorry, and then attacked them, inflicting severe casualties. He made use of this lorry on several occasions to render similar valuable and gallant service in the South of Ireland. Lt Hook also took a very distinguished part in the successful action against rebels at CLONMULT on the 20th February 1921.'

---

3   UKNA, Kew, WO 35/181, medal awards at Dublin Castle, 14th January 1922.
     Also, www.cairogang.com.
4   UKNA, Kew, WO 35/181, medal awards at Dublin Castle, 12th July 1921.
     Also, www.cairogang.com.

THE BATTLE OF CLONMULT (POEM)

On the 20th day of February in 1921,
Our noble Midleton heroes
Were murdered in Clonmult,
For the fighting of their country's cause
To free her they did go,
But by an informer of our land,
In their grave they're lying low.

The bravest boys in Ireland,
That house they did command,
Brave Desmond Brothers stood there,
True rebels to the last,
And many another mother's son
With hearts full grief did go,
To think that they should be betrayed
And their life's blood then left flow.

O'Hegarty you were a brave lad
And so was Ahern too,
Like the rest of the East Cork Martyrs
You were straight, firm and true,
Not forgetting Paddy Sullivan
And Moore as you now know
Who were executed in Cork Barracks,
And their life's blood then left flow.

'Twas on the Sabbath morning,
The district the 'Tans' did invade,
In search for Irish Rebels
Through many a hill and vale,
Surround were those boys at last
When rifle fire began,
And Desmond said-have courage lads
We have them nearly done.

From the top of roof and window
Those lads went on to fight,
With the burning of the cottage
Left no escape in sight,
But still they kept on fighting
Till they fell one by one,
And the sad news left old Midleton
That the column boys were done.

God rest those brave young heroes
And in heaven may they find rest,
And the flag of freedom flying o'er
The Churchyards where they rest,
For this sacrifice our noble boys-
T'is plainly to be seen,
They said they'd fight and even die
For the Yellow, White and Green.

CLONMULT'S LONELY VALE, FIRST VERSION (POEM)

This story I will tell you the truth I will unfold
About a group of volunteers who were betrayed for gold
Alas no more those lads we'll see their loss we now bewail
They bravely died for Ireland's cause in Clonmult's Lonely Vale.

About a score of fighting men, this column did command
They came from East Cork and Athlone our freedom to demand
Their shelter was a farm house well off the beaten trail
Beyond Dungourney village in Clonmult's Lonely Vale.

On a fine spring day in February the air was crisp and clear
When a Company of 'Black and Tans' and Hampshire's did appear
A traitor's information had set them on the trail
To the peaceful little farmhouse in Clonmult's Lonely Vale.

It was a Sunday evening late in the afternoon
The Volunteers were breaking camp they planned to march out soon
Two lads who went for water returned with an empty pail
When they heard the shout 'surrender' in Clonmult's Lonely Vale.

This call was swiftly answered with a volley in reply
We stand for our Republic we'll fight until we die
The Tans then set the roof ablaze while bullets flew like hail
And shot to death were twelve brave lads in Clonmult's Lonely Vale.

Now they lie in hallowed ground close by many a friend
Love of country was their crime their land they did defend
No foe they feared those Volunteers, true sons of the Gael
A prayer recite for those who died in Clonmult's Lonely Vale.

Dick Cashman

APPENDIX 18

CLONMULT'S LONELY VALE, SECOND VERSION (POEM)

Attend to me brave Irish men, attention young and old,
Of what I'm going to mention, the truth I now unfold,
Our Flying Corps, some are no more, their loss we now bewail,
For they nobly died for Ireland in Clonmult's Lonely Vale.

On the 20th day of February in the spring time of the year,
A company of Hampshire's in their lorries did appear,
Alas a base informer put those blood hounds on their trail,
To the farmhouse they occupied in Clonmult's Lonely Vale.

It was on a Sunday evening, late in the afternoon,
And little did they think that day that the fight would be so soon,
Those Volunteers they had no fear, being true sons of the Gael,
When they heard the cry surrender, in Clonmult's Lonely Vale.

They answered back defiantly and to them made the reply,
We're out for Irish freedom and we'll fight until we die,
They set the roof on fire and the bullets flew like hail,
In the farmhouse they occupied in Clonmult's Lonely Vale.

Through smoke and fire they did retire on to the kitchen floor,
Some of them were made prisoner, twelve left in their gore,
Their commander fled away from view and bounded o'er the dale,
And he shot down an officer in Clonmult's Lonely Vale.

And now my friends as I conclude, I think it's only fair,
Both old and young as we go along, for them we'll breathe a prayer,
And when the flag of freedom flies high o're Grainneuaile,
We should think with pride of the men who died in Clonmult's Lonely Vale.

Anon

APPENDIX 19

IN MEMORY OF THE BRAVE BOYS WHO FELL AT CLONMULT (POEM)

In the glory of manhood and strength they came
To fight for their cause and true,
And the patriot fire in each breast aflame
Blazed brightly for Roisín Dhú.

Stout hearts full of hope on that threshold stood
Which led to the fields of death,
For the fury of foemen around them brewed
They felt it in every breath.

But never a shadow of fear knew they
It was theirs but to do or die,
Theirs to fall in the hush of a springtide day
'Neath the blue of an Irish sky.

They are gone they're asleep in a martyr's grave
They have earned a martyr's crown,
Just one short year to-day their pure lives they gave
For love of Eire they laid them down.

But in letters of gold their names shall shine
Angels hover where oft' they've trod,
May they rest evermore in His realms divine
Those brave soldiers of Eire's sod.

(Mrs) Isabel Burke,
Rocksavage, Cork, 20th February 1922

IN CLONMULT'S VERDANT VALE (POEM)

Dedicated to the men who fell in the Battle of Clonmult, 20th February 1921

In the pale grey light of eventide,
'Neath Spring's first hopeful rays,
'Midst fragrant breath of heather bells
And songbirds' gladsome lays,
A battle grim and fierce was fought
'Neath the flag of Innisfail
Where Corrin's peak looks down
On Clonmult's verdant vale.

See yonder, o'er the heather clad slope
In battle's fierce array,
With hasty tread, with lightning speed
Like wolfhound on its prey,
With bayonets fixed rush Saxon men
The fence they quickly scale
And take their stand beside a cot
In Clonmult's verdant vale.

Why haste they thus, why gather round
This lonely wayside cot
Eark! Hear the challenge that rings out!
List the reply they got!
'Will you surrender?' Twice the cry,
Rings out upon the gale,
And twice the answer 'Never' sounds,
O'er Clonmult's verdant vale.

'Will you surrender' once again
This is the final word
For answer the flag of green floats high

All are to action stirred
Hear now the bomb and rifle sound
The bullets fall like hail
The battles din re-echoes loud
O'er Clonmult's verdant vale

'Neath Erin's flag those rebels fight
'Gainst forces of the Crown
Far better thus to die, than live
Beneath the tyrant's frown.
See! See the blaze! The roof's aflame
'Twould make a stout heart quail,
In Clonmult's verdant vale.

'Tis summer time on Corrin's slope
The songbirds are a trill'
Why gather there that concourse vast
Beside the heath clad hill
Tis sacred ground, this hallowed spot
A father old and frail,
A mother, sisters, brothers kneel
In Clonmult's verdant vale.

And we who gaze upon that scene
Where fell those heroes brave,
Can picture what a radiant light
There glows beyond the grave,
Where they now pray that Freedom's light
May dawn o'er Innisfail
And justify the stand they made
In Clonmult's verdant vale.

Sleep on, O gallant comrades, sleep,
You've won the martyr's crown,
And Erin's future sons will sing
Your deeds of fair renown.
When history's glorious pages tell
The wondrous, stirring tale,
All Gael's shall honour those who fell
In Clonmult's verdant vale.

Mr Michael Fitzgerald, Ballynoe

APPENDIX 21

THE OLD CAMP ON THE HILL (POEM)

Dramatic ballad of the Battle of Clonmult, 20th February 1921.
To the air of, 'A Highway for Freedom'.

O'er the lordly brow of Corrin Gael
The sun's pale rays are streaming
O'er valley steep and hillside grey
Many anxious eyes are gleaming,
Hear bomb and rifle peal
Re-echo loud around the hill,
And through the valley steal,
The foe is here, the fighting hard
To capture and to kill
The rebels brave who hold the fort –
The old camp on the hill.

As 'neath the crest of Corrin Gael
The sun sinks slowly down,
From vale and glen, from level plain,
And over hillside brown,
Come marching men, with souls a thrill
At duty's noble call,
To render aid to comrades true
With them to stand or fall,
To check the Saxon's onward march
The foe of Ireland still,
Too late, a blaze shoots upward from
The old camp on the hill.

The twilight shades are falling fast
O'er Corrin's lordly brow,
But brighter grows the brown hillside
The camp is blazing now!
What mortal frame can e'er withstand
Such fearsome deadly plight
But the rebel's bold keep fighting on
For Freedom and for Right.
Too well they know, as time has shown,
That traitor's cunning still
Has power to wreck for Saxon gold
The old camp on the hill.

Mr Michael Fitzgerald, Ballynoe

APPENDIX 22

DIARMUID O'HURLEY (POEM)

I will sing you the praise of a hero
An Irishman valiant and bold,
Who fought for the freedom of Ireland
Neath the flag of the green, white and gold.
Many is the battle he fought in
When victory his efforts did crown,
Sad now it is to say the bright month of May
By the Black and Tans he was shot down.

He fought for the freedom of Ireland
He died for the dear old land,
Unselfish, undaunted and daring
As any who gave a command.
'Comrades' said he, 'we will conquer and be free
A nation will be the result,'
As he laid them to rest the boys he loved best
Who fought and who died at Clonmult.

As he went out walking one evening
In order to take the fresh air,
By the banks of the clear shining river
The foes of our country were there.
They called him to halt and surrender
But he with a volley replied,
The Tans were there in great numbers
For the cause of his country he died.

His friends took his body that evening
And then at the close of next day,
When the sun from the heavens was leaving
To the chapel right over the way.
Where the bell gently peeled
and the people all kneeled,
For that hero of fame and renown
In silence and gloom he was laid in a tomb,
To rest for a while in Churchtown.

In the month of September, so charming
It is well I remember the day,
Five thousand in order were marching
How sadly our bands did play.
After Diarmuid's remains
Whose blood flowed in streams,
When he fought for old Ireland and you
In that dear sainted plot he will ne'er be forgot,
Where he sleeps with his comrades so true.

PRIMARY SOURCES AND INTERVIEWS

Unpublished Works

Ashe, B., *The Development of the IRA's Concepts of Guerrilla Warfare, 1917–1921*, M.A. Thesis, (U.C.C., 1996). Ref. DM 6328.

Borgonovo, J.M., *Informers, Intelligence and the 'Anti-Sinn Féin Society', The Anglo–Irish Conflict in Cork City, 1920–1921*, M.A. Thesis, (U.C.C., 1997). Ref. DM 5930.

Girvin, K.E., *The Life and Times of Sean O'Hegarty (1881–1963), O/C First Cork Brigade, War of Independence*, M. Phil. Thesis, (U.C.C., 2003). Ref. DM 7842.

Higgins, Patrick J., *The Story of Clonmult*, NLI, ref. MS 44,047/3, O'Mahony Papers.

Joy, S.M., *Co. Kerry, 1916–1921: A Provincial View of the IRA and The War of Independence*, M. Phil. Thesis, (U.C.C., 2000). Ref. DM 6796.

O'Donoghue papers, National Library of Ireland.

United Kingdom National Archives (UKNA), Kew, London

Clonmult Military Court case file, UKNA ref. WO 71/380.

Military Court of Inquiry in Lieu of Inquest, ref. Morrissey, WO 35/155A/53.

All twelve killed on 20 February in Clonmult are covered in the above.

Military Court of Inquiry in Lieu of Inquest, Jerh Hurley, WO 35/152/82.

Military Court of Inquiry in Lieu of Inquest, Wm Bransfield, WO 35/146B/12.

Military Court of Inquiry in Lieu of Inquest, RIC Const Webb, WO 35/160/54.

Military Court of Inquiry in Lieu of Inquest, Maurice Moore, WO 35/155B/18.

Military Court of Inquiry in Lieu of Inquest, Michael O'Keeffe, WO 35/157B/5.

Military Court of Inquiry in Lieu of Inquest, RIC Const M. Mullin, WO 35/155A/63.

Hampshire Regt., Clonmult after action report, WO 35/88B.

British Medal awards at Dublin Castle, 12 July 1921, WO 35/181.

Mourne Abbey, Military Court case file, UKNA, WO 71/386.

Bureau of Military History, 1913–21,

Individual Witness Statements,

Irish Military Archives, Cathal Brugha Bks, Dublin

Ahern, Eamon, Witness Statement No. 39.
Ahern, Comdt Joseph, Witness Statement No. 1367.
Buckley, (Bronco) William, Witness Statement No. 1009.
Burke, Capt Michael J., Witness Statement No. 1424.
Cashman, Daniel, Witness Statement No. 1523.
Coss, James, Witness Statement No. 1065.
Fitzgerald, Seamus, Witness Statement No. 1737.
Higgins, Capt Patrick J., Witness Statement No. 1467.
Hourihane, Thomas, Witness Statement No. 1366.
Kearney, Comdt Michael, Witness Statement No. 1418.
Kelleher, John, Witness Statement No. 1456.
Leahy, Comdt Michael, Witness Statement No. 94.
O'Connell, Lt Col John P., Witness Statement No. 1444.
O'Leary, Capt Diarmuid, Witness Statement No. 1589.
Whelan, Comdt Patrick J., Witness Statement No. 1449.

Primary Sources

Bureau of Military History, 1913–1921,

Statement by Witness

Ahern, Joseph,	Document No. 1367.
Burke, Michael J.,	Document No. 1424.
Cashman, Daniel,	Document No. 1523.
Fitzgerald, Seamus,	Document No. 1737.
Higgins, Patrick J.,	Document No. 1467.
Kelleher, John,	Document No. 1456.
Leahy, Michael,	Document No. 94.
O'Connell, John P.,	Document No. 1444.
O'Leary, Diarmuid,	Document No. 1589.
Whelan, Patrick, J.,	Document No. 1449.

U.K. National Archives, Kew, London.

Clonmult, Military-Court case file, WO 71/380.
Patrick Higgins, Military-Court case file, WO 83/41.
Military Court of Inquiry in Lieu of Inquest for Clonmult, WO/155A.
Military Court of Inquiry in Lieu of Inquest, Diarmuid Hurley, WO/35/152/82.
Military Court of Inquiry in Lieu of Inquest, Wm Bransfield, WO/35/146B/12.
Military Court of Inquiry in Lieu of Inquest, Maurice Moore, WO/35/155B/18.
Crown Forces Daily raids and reports, 12 Feb '21–10 Apr '21, WO/35/53.

Interviews

The late Mrs Theresa Cotter, Local (Carrigtwohill) historian interviewed by me March 2004.
The late Mr James Hegarty witnessed the battle, audio-taped interview with me, 7th December 2003 and 3rd March 2004.

Sources

C.A.I.	Cork Archives Institute
C.O.	Colonial Office
C.P.M.	Cork Public Museum
I.W.M.	Imperial War Museum, London
Mil. Arch.	Military Archives, Dublin
N.L.I.	National Library of Ireland
U.C.D., A.D.	U.C.D., Archive Department
U.K.N.A.	UK National Archives, Kew, London
W. S.	Witness Statement

BIBLIOGRAPHY

Published Works

Abbott, Richard, *Police Casualties in Ireland, 1919–1922*, Mercier Press, Cork, 2000, ISBN 1 85635 314 1.

Barry, Keane, *Cork's Revolutionary Dead, 1916–1923*, Mercier Press, Cork, 2017, ISBN 978-1-78117-495-1.

Barry, Michael B., *The Fight for Irish Freedom, An Illustrated History of the War of Independence*, Andalus Press, 2018, ISBN 978-0-9933554-6-2.

Barry, Tom, *Guerrilla Days in Ireland*, Irish Press Ltd., Dublin, 1949.

Barton, Brian, *From Behind a Closed Door, Secret Court Martial Records of the 1916 Easter Rising*, Blackstaff Press, Belfast, 2002, ISBN 0 85640 697 X.

Bennett, R., *The Black and Tans*, E. Hulton & Co. Ltd., London, 1959.

Breen, Dan, *My Fight for Irish Freedom*, Anvil Press, Tralee, 1975.

Brennan-Whitmore W.J., *With the Irish in Frongoch*, The Talbot Press, Dublin, 1917.

Carroll, Aideen, *Sean Moylan, Rebel Leader*, Mercier Press, Cork, 2010, ISBN 978 1 85635 669 5.

Cork County Council Heritage Unit, *Heritage Centenary Sites of Rebel County Cork*, Carrig Print Litho Press, County Cork, 2016, ISBN 978 0 9935969 1 9, PB, and ISBN 978 0 9935969 2 6, HB.

Cottrell, Peter, ed. *The War for Ireland, 1913–1923*, Osprey Publishing 2009, ISBN 978 1 84603 9966.

Defence Forces Printing Press, *Medals of the Irish Defence Forces*, First Edition 2010.

Enright, Sean, *The Trial of Civilians by Military Courts Ireland 1921*, Irish Academic Press, 2012, ISBN 978 0 7165 3133 3 (cloth) and ISBN 978 0 7165 3134 0 (paper).

Falvey, Jeremiah, *The Chronicles of Midleton 1700–1990*, Sira Publications, Cloyne, Co. Cork, 1998, ISBN 0 9534650 0 4.

Feeneey, P.J., *Glory O, Glory O, Ye Bold Fenian Men*, Dripsey, Co. Cork, 1996.

Fitzgerald, Seamus, East Cork Activities 1920, *The Capuchin Annual, 1970*, pp. 360–368.

Foxton, David, *Revolutionary Lawyers, Sinn Féin Courts in Ireland and Britain 1916–1923*, Four Courts Press, 2008, ISBN 978-1-84682-068-7.

Hanley, Brian, *A Guide to Irish Military Heritage*, Four Courts Press, Maynooth Research Guides for Irish Local History, number 7, 2004, ISBN 1 85182 788 9, hardback and ISBN 1 85182 789 7, paperback.

Hart, Peter, *The IRA and its Enemies, Violence and Community in Cork, 1916–1923*, Oxford University Press, 1998, ISBN 0-19-820537-6.

Hart, Peter, *The IRA at War 1916–1923*, Oxford University Press, 2003, ISBN 0 19 925258 0.

Hart, Peter (ed.), *British Intelligence in Ireland, 1920–21, The Final Reports*, Cork University Press, 2002, ISBN 1 85918 201 1.

Harvey, D. and White, G., *The Barracks, A History of Victoria/Collins Barracks, Cork*, Mercier Press, Cork, 1997, ISBN 1 85635 194 7.

Hogan, David, (pseudo. Frank Gallagher), *The Four Glorious Years*, Irish Press Ltd., Dublin, 1953.

Hogan, Sean, *The Black and Tans in South Tipperary, Policing, Revolution and War, 1913–1922*. Guardian Print & Design, Nenagh, Co. Tipperary, 2013. ISBN 1 901370 45 4.

Hopkinson, Michael, *The Irish War of Independence*, Gill and Macmillan, Dublin, 2002, ISBN 0 7171 3010 X.

Jeffers, John, *Death on the Pier*, Lettertec Publishing, 2017, no ISBN.

Keane, Barry, *Cork's Revolutionary Dead 1916–1923*, Mercier Press, Cork, 2017, ISBN 978 1 78117 495 1.

Killeagh-Inch Historical Group, *Killeagh Parish Throughout the Ages*.

Macardle, Dorothy, *The Irish Republic*, Irish Press Ltd, Dublin, 1951.

MacEoin, Uinseann, *Survivors*, Argenta Publications, Dublin, 1980.

McCall, Ernest, *Tudor's Toughs, The Auxiliaries, 1920–1922*, Red Coat Publishing, Newtownards, Co. Down, 2010, ISBN 978-0-9538367-3-4.

McCall, Ernest, *The Auxies, 1920–1922, A Pictorial History*, Red Coat Publishing, Newtownards, Co. Down, 2013, ISBN 978-0-9538367-5-8.

McCall, Ernest, *The First Anti-Terrorist Unit, The Auxiliary Division, RIC*, Red Coat Publishing, Newtownards, Co. Down, 2018, ISBN 978-0-9538367-6-5.

McCann, John, Thirty Pieces of Silver, in, *War by the Irish*, The Kerryman, Tralee, 1946.

McCarthy, Cal, *Cumann na mBan and the Irish Revolution*, revised edition, The Collins Press, Cork, 2014, ISBN 9781848892224.

McCarthy, Kieran/Christensen, Maj-Britt, *Cobh's Contribution to the Fight for Irish Freedom, 1913–1990*, Oileann Mór Publications, Cobh, Co. Cork, 1992.

Maher, Jim, *The Flying Column of West Kilkenny, 1916–1921*, Geography Publications, Dublin, first edition 1988, PB, no ISBN.

Maher, Jim, *The Flying Column of West Kilkenny, 1916–1921*, Geography Publications, Dublin, second edition 2015, ISBN 978-0-906602-683, HB.

Maxwell, Henry, T., *The Irish Reports, 1921, Vol. 2, The King's Bench Division*, The Incorporated Council of Law Reporting for Ireland, Dublin, 1921.

Monthly [British] Army List 1921, A distribution List of Officers on the Active List of the Regular Army, the Royal Marines, H.M. Stationary Office, London.

Moore, Tony, *Clonmult and the Construction of a Legend*, A Dissertation for Consideration by the University of Humberside as part of the B.A. (Honours) Degree in Combined Studies, 1996.

Murphy, Gerard, *The Year of Disappearances, Political Killings in Cork 1921–1922*, Gill and Macmillan, Dublin, 2010, ISBN 978 07171 4748 9.

Murphy, Sean, A. *Kilmichael, A Battlefield Study*, Four Roads Publications, 2014, ISBN 978 0 9931164 0 7.

Murphy, William, *Political Imprisonment & the Irish, 1912–1921*, Oxford University Press, 2014, ISBN 978-0-19-956907-6.

National Graves Association, *The Last Post, Details and Stories of Irish Republican Dead, 1916–1985*, Elo Press, Dublin, 1985.

O'Callaghan, Sean, *Execution*, Frederick Muller Limited, London, 1974.

O'Ciosain, Padraig, Operations in East Cork, *Rebel Corks Fighting Story from 1916 to the Truce with Britain*, Anvil Press 1947.

O'Donoghue, Florence, *No Other Law*, Irish Press Ltd, Dublin, 1954.

O'Donoghue, Florence, *Tomás Mac Curtain*, The Kerryman Ltd., Tralee, 1958.

O'Farrell, Padraic, *Who's Who in the Irish War of Independence 1916–1921*, The Mercier Press, Dublin and Cork, 1980, ISBN 0 85342 604 6.

O'Mahony, Sean, *Frongoch, University of Revolution*, FDR Teoranta, Dublin, 1987.

O'Sullivan, John L., *Cork City Gaol*, Ballyheada Press 1996, no ISBN.

O'Toole, E.H., *Decorations and Medals of the Republic of Ireland*, Medallic Publishing Company, Connecticut, 1990, ISBN 0 9624663 5.

Kerryman, *With the IRA in the Fight for Freedom 1919 to the Truce, the Red Path of Glory*, Kerryman, Tralee, n.d.

Kerryman, *Rebel Cork's Fighting Story, from 1916 to the Truce with Britain*, Kerryman edition, n.d.

Kerryman, *Rebel Cork's Fighting Story, from 1916 to the Truce with Britain*, Anvil Edition, The Kerryman, Tralee, n.d.

Kingston, Diarmuid, *Beleaguered: A History of the RIC in West Cork during the War of Independence*. Diarmuid Kingston 2013. ISBN 978-0-9927223-0-2.

Lenihan, Michael, *Cork Burning*, Mercier Press, Cork, 2018, ISBN 978 1 78117 6245.

Ryan, Annie, *Comrades, Inside the War of Independence*, Liberties Press, Dublin, 2007, ISBN 978-1-905483-14-3 PB, ISBN 978-1-905483-22-8, HB,

Scott Daniell, David, *The Regimental History of the Royal Hampshire Regiment*, Gale and Polden, Aldershot, 1955, Vol. 3, 1918–1954.

Sheehan, Tim, *Lady Hostage*, Dripsey Press, Co. Cork, 1990.

Sheehan, William, *British Voices from the Irish War of Independence, 1918–1921*, The Collins Press, Cork, 2005, ISBN -10: 1903464897.

Townshend, Charles, *The British Campaign in Ireland 1919–1921, The Development of Political and Military Policies*, Oxford University Press, 1975.

Twohig, Canon Patrick J., *Green Tears for Hecuba*, Tower Books, Ballincollig, Co. Cork, 1994, ISBN 0 902568 23 X.

White, G., and O'Shea, B., *The Irish Volunteer Soldier 1913–23*, Osprey Publishing, Warrior Series No. 80, Wellingborough, Northants, U.K., 2003, ISBN 1 84176 685 2.

White, G., and O'Shea, B., *Baptised in Blood, the formation of the Cork Brigade of the Irish Volunteers 1913–1916*, Mercier Press, Cork, 2005, ISBN 1 85635 465 2.

White, G., and O'Shea, B., *The Burning of Cork*, Mercier Press, Cork, 2006, ISBN 1 85635 522 5/ 978 85635 522 3.

INDEX

Hammond, H, Lt 35, 36, 40, 46, 48, 67, 69, 70–2, 123, 127, 130, 131, 133, 136, 137

Hampshire Regt 8, 34, 35, 58, 66, 68–70, 104, 122, 125–28, 130, 132, 134, 136, 149

Harris, Henry, RIC 45, 70, 127

Harty, John 29, 40, 47–9, 54, 65, 66, 69, 70, 74–8, 85, 87, 95, 110, 119, 122, 123

Harty, Margaret 77

Hayes, Jack 98

Hegarty, Jim 8, 55

Hegarty, Mary 58

Hegarty, Richard 29, 30, 40, 42, 44, 49, 58, 61, 74, 75, 77, 78, 83, 84, 107, 119, 120, 122–3

Henderson, K R, Lt 104

Hendy, R A, Lt 104

Hennessy, Kate 76

Higgins, Patrick 8, 13, 20, 31–3, 38, 42, 44, 46, 47–9, 53, 54, 62, 64, 66, 95, 98, 106–10, 119, 120, 123, 149–51

Higginson, H.W., Col 98, 125, 129

Holy Rosary Cemetery 104

Hook, DF, Lt 35–7, 42, 43, 44, 47, 48, 68, 72, 122, 123, 125, 127, 130–1, 137

House of Lords 108, 109

Hyde, Jack 120

Hyde, Philip 99, 120

Hyde, Tom 120

Joyce, John, Joe 40, 41, 49, 59, 67, 119, 120, 123

Joyce, Mary 59

Kearney, Michael 121, 150

Keeffe, Patrick 103

Kelleher, John 120, 150

Kennedy, H. K.C. 108

Kilbrittain 90

Kilgobnait 105

Killacloyne 51

Killeagh 14, 15, 42, 65, 83, 88, 119, 120

Kilmichael 46, 48, 49, 113

Kilmountain, Midleton 19, 20, 122

Kilnadur, Dunmanway 14

King's Bench Division 86

Kinsella, Joe 54

Knockraha 14, 17, 19, 50, 51, 52, 122

Koe, AR, Lt 35, 36, 40, 41, 43, 47, 69, 71, 72, 115, 123, 127, 130–3, 137

Ladysbridge 14, 15, 19, 26, 30, 58, 59, 74, 78, 83

Lawton, Johnny 50

Leahy, Mick 12, 97, 118, 150

Leamlara 14, 28, 32, 51, 53

Leinster Regt 79

Lindsay, Mary 89, 90

Lord Lieutenant 63, 65, 87–8

Lynch, K.C. 108

Lynch, Liam 14

MacCurtain. T, 11, 12, 14

Macready, N, General 64, 66, 87–8, 109–10, 125

Macroom 104–5

Mackey, Nellie 59

MacSwiney, Terence 12

Manley, Tadhg 17

Mantle, S E T, Sgt 70, 127

Martial Law 46, 63–66, 69, 73, 86–8, 108–9, 112, 128, 136

Masterson, Dick 98